THE **LOOK** OF **SUCCESS**

Redefining Achievement, Identity,
and Fulfillment on Your Own Terms

DR. KARISSA THOMAS

The Look of Success: Redefining Achievement, Identity, and Fulfillment on Your Own Terms

By Dr. Karissa Thomas

First Edition: 2014

Updated Edition: 2026

Visit our website at: themosaicleader.com

Library of Congress Control Number: 2025911576

ISBN: 978-1-968277-08-6

Interior Design: Marigold Emal

Printed in the United States of America

I dedicate this book to the Russian writer Leo Tolstoy
(September 9, 1828 – November 20, 1910).

Tolstoy was a man unafraid to embody his own look of success, even
amid the controversy that often surrounded his work. True to his
calling as a writer, the integrity of his art mattered more to him than
society's approval or resistance. He chose truth over comfort, conviction over conformity, and purpose over praise.

More than a century after his passing, I can say with clarity and
conviction: you owned your look of success, Tolstoy.

ADIEU TO A SOLDIER

by Walt Whitman (May 31, 1819 – March 26, 1892)

Adieu, O soldier!
You of the rude campaigning (which we shared),
The rapid march, the life of the camp,
The hot contention of opposing fronts—
The long maneuver,
Red battles with their slaughter—
The stimulus—the strong, terrific game,

Spell of all brave and manly hearts—
The trains of Time through you, and the like of you, all filled
With war, and war's expression.

Adieu, dear comrade!
Your mission is fulfilled—but I, more warlike,
Myself, and this contentious soul of mine,
Still on our own campaigning bound,
Through untried roads, with ambushes, opponents lined,
Through many a sharp defeat and many a crisis—often baffled,
Here marching, ever marching on, a war to fight out—aye, here,
To fiercer, weightier battles give expression.

This book was originally written in 2014, during a very different season of my life and at a markedly different moment in the world. It predates the rise of influencer culture, the normalization of remote work, and the era in which productivity, visibility, and worth became increasingly entangled. It was written before constant connectivity reshaped how we measure success, before burnout became a shared language, and before many people began questioning whether the lives they were building truly reflected who they were becoming.

For this edition, I chose not to rewrite the book, but to refine it. That decision was intentional. While the external landscape has shifted dramatically, the core message of this work remains unchanged: meaningful success begins internally. Before titles, before validation, before strategy or recognition, there must be clarity, self-trust, and an honest understanding of what success actually means to you.

Readers will encounter the voice and perspective of an earlier season—direct, reflective, and grounded in substance rather than performance. Some passages may feel quieter than today's content culture encourages, slower than the pace of modern consumption. That restraint is not accidental. It reflects a way of thinking that values depth over immediacy and alignment over acceleration.

This edition is offered as a bridge across generations. It speaks to those navigating ambition in an age of constant comparison, to professionals and leaders redefining success beyond exhaustion, and to individuals who sense that achievement without integrity ultimately costs more than it delivers. The questions explored in these pages remain relevant because the work of self-definition is timeless, even as the context continues to evolve.

If you are reading this book during a season of transition—personally, professionally, or internally—consider this an invitation rather than a prescription. You are not behind. You are not failing. You are in the process of becoming more intentional about how you live, lead, and measure progress.

My hope is that this book meets you where you are, while also encouraging you to slow down, reflect, and take control of your own definition of success. Clarity continues to be a form of power. Self-trust remains a skill worth developing. And the most lasting success, in any era, is still built from the inside out.

—Dr. Karissa Thomas

WHO THIS BOOK IS FOR

This book is for those who sense that success is more complex than achievement alone.

It is for readers who have reached milestones yet still feel misaligned, fatigued, or quietly questioning whether the life they are building truly reflects who they are becoming. It is for individuals who understand that outward success, without internal clarity, often comes at a hidden cost.

This book is for professionals, leaders, creatives, educators, and entrepreneurs who are willing to examine their relationship with time, money, motivation, and identity—and who recognize that sustainable success requires more than effort or ambition. It requires self-awareness, discipline, and the courage to define success on one's own terms.

It is for those navigating transition: a career shift, a personal recalibration, a season of loss, or a moment of internal reckoning. If you are rebuilding, refining, or redefining what success means to you, this book was written with you in mind.

This book is not a step-by-step formula, a shortcut, or a motivational performance. It does not promise instant results or external validation. Instead, it offers a framework for reflection, responsibility, and intentional growth. Readers who are seeking depth over hype, alignment over acceleration, and clarity over comparison will find resonance here.

Ultimately, this book is for those who are ready to stop measuring success by appearances alone—and to begin carrying it with integrity, awareness, and purpose.

If you are reading this book during a season of transition, know that you are not lost—you are in motion.

Life transitions often arrive quietly. Sometimes they come with disruption, loss, or uncertainty. Sometimes they appear as restlessness, dissatisfaction, or a subtle knowing that the life you have been living no longer fits the person you are becoming. These moments can feel destabilizing, but they are also deeply instructive.

Transition does not mean failure. It does not mean you made the wrong choices or fell behind. It means your internal compass is recalibrating. Growth often requires the release of outdated roles, identities, or definitions of success before something more aligned can take shape.

This book was written for those moments—when certainty is gone, but clarity has not yet arrived. You do not need to have all the answers to move forward. You only need the willingness to ask better questions, sit with discomfort long enough to learn from it, and trust that your next chapter does not require you to become someone new—only more honest about who you already are.

If you are rebuilding, redefining, or beginning again, allow yourself patience. Allow yourself to reflect. Success, when built with integrity, often emerges from these in-between spaces.

This book is not a promise of immediate resolution. It is an invitation to move through transition with intention, self-respect, and courage—so that what comes next is not simply successful, but sustainable.

CONTENTS

by Kathleen Thomas

This book is especially meaningful to me—not only because my daughter wrote it, but because many people misunderstand what it truly takes to be successful. When I reflect on my own life, I recognize that few can fully see what it required—often carried alone—to build the life I envisioned. People see outcomes, not effort. They see results, not the discipline, doubt, and persistence that make those results possible.

There was a time early in my life when success appeared visible and immediate. I was crowned Miss Trinidad in 1978, a moment that brought recognition, opportunity, and attention. From the outside, it looked like arrival. From the inside, it marked the beginning of a much more complex journey. Life shifted quickly. Expectations followed. And I learned early that visibility does not equal security, and recognition does not guarantee stability.

What followed was not a straight path upward, but a series of choices that required grounding, sacrifice, and endurance. I learned that success must be carried, not worn. It demands internal capacity long after external applause fades. Titles pass. Seasons change. What remains is the strength you build beneath the surface.

I believe success has always existed within me. We come from a Source of abundance, and no circumstance can take that away. When I consider what success has meant across my life—not in one moment, but over time—one word consistently rises: sacrifice. Not as punishment, but as intention. To pursue success, something must be exchanged—comfort, immediacy, certainty. Nothing meaningful arrives without cost, and not all costs are visible to others.

Many people want success, but they want it without the work it requires. That was never my story. Nothing was handed to me. I earned what I have through discipline, restraint, and long-term vision. Still, people often say, "I'm not worried about you—you'll be alright," as if success has always come easily. That assumption usually reflects how little of the journey is truly seen.

I was not born into wealth. I did not have a silver spoon. I had a vision—and I made deliberate sacrifices to pursue it. I chose less in the short term so that more would be possible later. I paid for my education as I went, so I would not carry debt forward. I made financial choices that required discipline, so my daughter could pursue the education she desired. I built a business through consistency, not convenience. There were seasons when I postponed comfort, variety, and ease in order to protect the larger picture. Today, I enjoy what was once delayed—not because it was owed to me, but because it was planned for.

What I have learned is that success requires a strong foundation. Vision matters, but commitment sustains it. Achievement alone is not the goal. The greater challenge is developing the capacity to hold responsibility, pressure, and progress without losing balance or self-respect.

There were times when I worked for wages far below what reflected my effort or ability—not because I accepted less of myself, but because I understood the tradeoffs of that season. There were also moments in my personal life when choices were difficult, and options felt limited. Those experiences taught me an unspoken truth about success: it does not remove struggle. It refines judgment. It strengthens resolve. It demands responsibility.

I hope this book reaches those who see themselves as "unfortunate," those who believe success is out of reach or reserved for others. I want them to understand that they already possess what they need to begin. But I also want them to know this truth—the journey will test you. At times, it will feel unclear or unfair. Still, trust that growth is occurring, even when progress feels slow. In time, understanding reveals itself.

Sometimes we focus so intensely on what was lost that we overlook what is being built. I share this with confidence because I continue to experience it myself. Each year, I learn more. Each year, I lose more weight. Fulfillment deepens not because life becomes easier, but because understanding becomes clearer. We forgive ourselves for what we once carried, recognizing how necessary it was for who we are becoming.

You never stop learning. You never stop growing. With time comes perspective. With perspective comes wisdom. We are evolving beings, and success must evolve with us.

In this book, Karissa offers thoughtful insight into what it truly takes to succeed—not just to achieve, but to sustain. Always remember: reaching a goal is only the beginning. The greater work is learning how to carry success with clarity, balance, and purpose. Motivation endures when it is rooted in self-understanding, not comparison.

> "Better go home and make
> a net, rather than dive
> for fish at random."
> —Chinese Proverb

Many people seek success, yet they are often unsure how to achieve it. One reason is simple: success does not mean the same thing to everyone. Its definition shifts depending on where a person is in life, what they value, and what they are trying to build. What one individual considers success may look entirely different to someone else.

A subordinate may look at a senior manager and define success by position or title. A peer may focus on visible markers—a respected career, a large home, a luxury vehicle, a carefully curated wardrobe, or designer jewelry. Others may view entrepreneurial wealth as the ultimate sign of success. Beneath all these interpretations, however, lies a deeper, quieter question many people ask themselves: *What do I need to do to become successful?*

In truth, what they are often asking is more complex. How do I set meaningful goals? How do I achieve them? Can those goals generate income so I can afford the life I want? From there, an assumption quietly forms: if I have everything I want, then I must be successful.

But this is the distinction few people make—following a plan and achieving a goal does not automatically lead to fulfillment or happiness.

Success need not remain a distant dream, nor is it reserved for a select few. It is not something you must wait for, fantasize about, or hope will arrive someday. You can achieve success. You deserve success. It is not exclusive; you already have the capacity to create what your heart desires.

In many ways, the mystery has already been solved. Too often, people conceal their journey to success, as if sharing the truth might diminish what they have gained. But success is not about guarding secrets. It is about creating a plan that supports your growth while remaining aligned with your values and mindful of others. It is about allowing your vision to expand without losing your integrity. We come from a wellspring of abundance, and access to it is not limited.

People frequently attribute success to luck. I have never belonged to any exclusive circle of "lucky" individuals, so I cannot speak to that idea. What I do know is that timing matters. What some call luck is often timing paired with preparation. We all encounter the same winds—the winds of opportunity and the winds of adversity. What determines the outcome is how we choose to set our sails.

You can create your own success, just as I have. Yes, some people are born with financial advantages, physical advantages, or an early head start. But comparison is misleading. You never truly know what someone has endured to arrive where they are—or what it costs them internally to maintain that position. Hopefully, they have found peace somewhere along the way.

Judging success from the outside leads to assumptions that rarely serve anyone. We observe without context, form opinions without understanding, and measure lives without knowing the full story. These judgments do nothing to alter another person's reality, nor do they deepen our own.

We have all witnessed lives that appeared extraordinarily successful from the outside—admired, celebrated, financially secure—yet marked by deep internal suffering. Public recognition often conceals private strain. The world sees achievement, but it does not always see the emotional cost of sustaining it.

This raises a question few discussions of success address: what does it mean to achieve something your inner life is not prepared to carry?

Success has layers. There is wanting it, achieving it, sustaining it, and learning how to pursue it in ways that are emotionally sustainable.

Most people live between desire and achievement, unaware that success isn't only about wanting and doing. It also involves maintenance—the pressure, expectations, and emotional weight that come with achievement. Success can shape you, and if you're not prepared for it, it can also break you. You must learn how to survive success—not just chase it. The pressure that comes with reaching your goals can threaten your ability to enjoy what you've worked so hard to build.

You have likely heard the phrase, "Be careful what you wish for—you just might get it." My version is this: be intentional in how you define success, and be strong enough to carry it once it arrives.

When someone sits down to write a guide to success, there are many layers to consider. At its core, success has a beginning, a middle, and an evolution. This book focuses on that process—the journey itself.

Wanting success is the first step. Achieving it is the second. Learning how to live with it is where most people falter.

The formula appears simple: time, energy, determination, and action. But simplicity should never be mistaken for ease. This process challenges more than the body; it challenges the spirit. We are more than physical beings. What sustains us are the quiet internal forces—desire, intuition, purpose, and drive. Yet it is the body, through action, that brings those forces into reality.

To understand success, you must first understand yourself. The deeper your self-awareness, the more grounded and enduring your success will become.

Throughout this book, success is not seen as a destination, status, or finish line. It is viewed as capacity—the inner ability to manage responsibility, visibility, pressure, choice, and change without losing coherence. Success isn't measured by what you gain, but by what you can sustain. When capacity grows, success feels more achievable. When capacity is overwhelmed, even accomplishments can become destabilizing. This book explores how capacity is built, tested, refined, and honored over a lifetime.

PREPARING YOUR MIND FOR SUCCESS

> **"**
>
> *"He who would learn to fly one day must first learn to stand and walk and run and dance; one cannot fly into flying."*
> —Friedrich Nietzsche
>
> **"**

Congratulations on taking the first step toward defining success on your own terms. Before anything else changes in your life—before opportunities arise, doors open, or results become clear—your mindset needs to be in the right place. The way you view success will shape not only what you go after but also how you experience it when it comes.

If you are reading this book during a season of transition, pause here for a moment. You are not late. You are not behind. You are not broken. You are in a recalibration phase—one that often precedes meaningful change.

Transitions rarely announce themselves clearly. Sometimes they come through loss: a job ending, a relationship dissolving, a role shifting, a chapter closing sooner than expected. Other times, they arrive quietly—like dissatisfaction, restlessness, or the feeling that the life you're living no longer reflects the person you're becoming. In either case, transition creates uncertainty. And uncertainty demands clarity of mind.

This book is designed to meet you there.

Before moving forward, it is important to ask a simple question: **Is this book the right fit for you?**

If you have read my other work, including *Foolproof: A Woman's Guide to Self-Love, Strength, and Relationships* or *Uncertainty to Confidence: A New Way of Living Your Life*, you will notice that *The Look of Success* takes a different approach. This book is more focused and more practical. It is not centered on inspiration alone; it is designed to help you understand your personal relationship with success and engage with it intentionally—especially when your direction feels unclear.

If you are familiar with my writing, you know that I do not soften reality or sell illusions. Real change begins with honesty, not fantasy. I do not write to offer shortcuts or promises of motivation. I write to challenge your thinking, because sustainable success requires mental discipline before momentum.

This book is for those who are willing to pause long enough to ask better questions.

As you pursue success—or if you're already on the path—you'll quickly see that no one can walk it for you. The journey is yours alone. Not only must you walk it, but you must also find it. During times of change, this can feel especially lonely. Old structures break down. Previous identities no longer fit. External validation may vanish just when you need reassurance the most.

That does not mean you are failing. It means you are being asked to develop internal authority.

There is no universal roadmap. Every path looks different. Some are steep and obstructed; others appear smoother on the outside but carry hidden costs. Either way, the responsibility for interpreting the terrain and pressing forward rests with you.

Along the way, you will face trade-offs. You will ask yourself difficult questions:

Am I on the right path?
Do I want to continue this way?
Should I pivot or adjust course?

These questions are not signs of weakness. They are signs of awareness.

To navigate them, you will need practical survival tools—education, resilience, adaptability, emotional regulation, and strategic thinking. In today's interconnected world, relationships and networks matter, but progress is rarely linear. At times, it will feel like two steps forward and one step back. Transition amplifies that feeling. No one promised that success—or reinvention—would be easy.

Success takes time. It requires sustained effort, discipline, emotional control, and clarity of thought. It involves financial decisions, motivation, skill development, setbacks, and persistence. Above all, it requires mental toughness—the ability to stay grounded as your circumstances take shape.

Your mind must be prepared before meaningful achievement can take root. Too often, people approach growth with entitlement rather than readiness—demanding outcomes, expecting ease, and growing frustrated when progress unfolds slowly. During periods of transition, that frustration often turns inward, becoming self-doubt. This book exists to interrupt that pattern.

There is no shortage of so-called formulas for success, many of which oversimplify or mislead. You may have heard advice such as, "Change your friends—surround yourself with successful people and success will follow." While appealing, this idea ignores reality. You cannot simply enter someone else's circle. Communities are formed with intention, boundaries, and shared values. Access is earned, not assumed—and not every circle is aligned with your purpose or your current season.

True growth begins internally. Especially during transition, external strategies fail without internal alignment. You must desire success for yourself and commit to your own development—even when the outcome is not yet visible. When inner transformation occurs, you begin to generate the kind of mental and emotional energy that opens doors. You learn how to create paths where none previously existed.

Some readers wonder why this book doesn't focus on just one area of success, such as money or relationships. The answer is simple: once you grasp the principles of success, you can apply them anywhere. This isn't a textbook on investing or business tactics. It's a guide to building the mindset, discipline, and resilience needed to succeed in any area you choose—especially when you're rebuilding, redefining, or starting fresh.

Success is a process. Once you understand that process, you can repeat it.

Whether your goal is to launch a business, complete your education, rebuild after loss, redefine your career, restore your confidence, or simply regain clarity during a season of transition, the foundation remains the same: learn continuously, develop yourself, take action, evaluate honestly, adjust when necessary, and keep moving forward.

This book is a place to regroup.

A place to think clearly.

A place to prepare—before you fly.

That is how you define—and ultimately live—your look of success.

CHAPTER ONE

WHAT IS THE LOOK OF SUCCESS?

> 66
>
> *"It is in exchanging the gifts of the earth that you shall find abundance and be satisfied. Yet unless the exchange be in love and kindly justice, it will but lead some to greed and others to hunger."*
>
> —Kahlil Gibran
>
> 99

The Question Beneath the Question

Most people believe they are pursuing success. In reality, they often seek legitimacy—validation that their lives, choices, and sacrifices are justified within frameworks they didn't consciously select. From a young age, individuals are exposed to powerful images of what success is supposed to look like, shaped by culture, economics, visibility, and reward. These images are rarely questioned. Over time, they solidify into internal standards that quietly influence decisions long before awareness develops.

This book starts with a deceptively simple question: What does success truly look like when no one is watching? Not what earns applause or photographs easily, nor what signals arrival to others, but what remains when external validation disappears. This difference is important because many people spend years chasing outcomes that seem impressive from the outside but feel increasingly out of sync internally.

Defining Success on Your Own Terms

The appearance of success isn't the same for everyone, fixed, or handed down entirely. It is influenced by age, life stage, responsibility, opportunity, loss, endurance, and the personal negotiations people make with themselves about what they are willing to bear—and what they are no longer willing to pretend matters. What signifies success to one person may seem hollow or burdensome to another, not because one definition is better, but because each life develops within different limits and values.

For some, success is highly visible and externally validated—such as financial security, professional status, influence, access, or recognition. These markers are not inherently shallow; they often reflect discipline, risk, and sustained effort. For others, success is quieter and less performative: emotional steadiness, autonomy, health, integrity, meaningful contribution, or the ability to live without constant internal strain. The mistake occurs when success is viewed as a universal template rather than a contextual truth.

Success is not competitive. It is relative to circumstances and measured internally before being displayed externally. A recovering addict may define success as sobriety and structure. A first-generation college graduate may see it as a source of stability and access. An executive might view it as alignment, boundaries, or the freedom to step back without collapsing. Each definition carries weight because success that is not internally coherent eventually loses its meaning, no matter how impressive it appears to others.

The Cost of Unexamined Success

Many people achieve what they were told to want, only to realize that fulfillment doesn't come automatically. The discomfort that appears at this point is often mistaken for burnout or ingratitude, but it actually signifies a deeper reflection. After earning credentials, gaining titles, and reaching milestones, a necessary question arises: Is this life truly mine?

This moment isn't a failure. It's awareness arriving late—but arriving nonetheless. When success is chased without reflection, it can quietly demand sacrifices that go unnoticed until alignment breaks down. What once motivated begins to drain. What once inspired now feels obligatory. The cost isn't always visible, but it accumulates over time.

Success After Disruption

For many people, the most truthful definition of success is not discovered during growth, but during upheaval. Illness, loss, divorce, public failure, career collapse, financial troubles, grief, or emotional exhaustion disrupt momentum and take away performance. These experiences prompt reevaluation. They show which goals were driven by fear, which identities were formed for approval, and which pursuits can no longer withstand honest self-reflection.

In these seasons, success often appears smaller but more precise. Recovery counts as progress. Stability is an achievement. Regaining clarity becomes a form of success itself. This is not regression; it is reconstruction. Disruption does not disqualify a person from success — it reshapes its definition.

Recovery isn't a detour from success; it's often the gateway to a more sustainable one. Those who recover after disruption often emerge with sharper priorities, stronger boundaries, and a clearer understanding of what they are—and are not—willing to sacrifice to achieve. Success that follows disruption tends to last longer because it's no longer just aspirational showmanship. It's rooted in real, lived experience.

The Invitation of This Book

This book is not meant to dismantle ambition. It aims to discipline it—separating desire from conditioning, growth from accumulation, and alignment from inherited momentum. The appearance of success isn't something to chase blindly. It's something to clarify intentionally.

That clarification, when undertaken honestly, changes everything that follows.

Success as a Personal Vision

Your look of success begins as a vision—one that belongs to you alone. It is not borrowed from social expectations, cultural pressure, family assumptions, or comparison. It emerges through reflection, honesty, and lived experience, shaped by the questions you are willing to ask yourself when external voices fall quiet. This vision is deeply personal, and its power lies in the fact that it cannot be replicated or outsourced.

That vision is not static. It evolves as you do. What you want at twenty-five may bear little resemblance to what you need at forty-five. What once felt aspirational may later feel constraining. Success matures alongside identity, responsibility, and awareness. Like any long-term strategy, it requires periodic reassessment. Growth demands adjustment, not rigidity.

Many people struggle not because they lack ambition, discipline, or talent, but because they are pursuing versions of success that were never truly theirs. When goals are misaligned with values, progress becomes draining rather than sustaining. Effort increases while meaning diminishes. Achievement without alignment does not produce fulfillment; it produces exhaustion.

When success is defined internally—grounded in values rather than validation—it becomes steadier and more resilient. It no longer requires constant comparison to justify its worth. It endures change, adapts to transition, and supports long-term well-being rather than undermining it.

Bridging the Vision to the Path

A personal vision of success offers direction, but vision alone does not establish stability. Without structure, even the clearest definition of success remains aspirational—felt, but not yet experienced. To shift from intention to reality, success must be viewed not as a single achievement but as an ongoing developmental process.

Success rarely comes fully formed. It develops in stages—each one essential, each one a learning opportunity. These stages aren't fixed steps to rush or check off. They are growth milestones. Skipping a stage might accelerate short-term gains, but it can create vulnerabilities that emerge later under pressure.

Understanding these phases helps you honestly identify where you are in the process, rather than judging progress by external timelines or comparisons. The goal isn't speed; it's sustainability.

The Seven Phases of Success

Mental Readiness

Success begins with mental clarity. This phase requires examining beliefs about success, worth, and capability. It demands honesty about current circumstances, internal resistance, and unexamined assumptions. Without mental readiness, progress collapses under pressure because unaddressed beliefs eventually override intention.

Vision Development

Once mental clarity is established, you define what success looks like for you. Early vision is often incomplete or abstract, and that is expected. Over time, clarity sharpens. This phase requires imagination paired with realism—acknowledging your starting point without allowing it to define your ceiling.

Skill Building

Vision without preparation creates frustration. This phase demands learning, practice, discipline, and humility. You develop the skills required for your chosen direction, often through repetition rather than inspiration. Competence builds confidence, and confidence sustains momentum when motivation fluctuates.

Strategic Positioning

At this stage, you begin to position yourself closer to opportunities. This includes awareness of environments, industries, systems, and relationships that support growth. Roles, responsibilities, and projects—especially those that feel temporary or imperfect—become part of your education. Nothing is wasted when it is understood as positioning.

Execution and Discipline

Here, success stops being theoretical. Action becomes consistent, and discipline replaces motivation. You invest time, energy, and focus—often without immediate recognition or reward. This phase tests commitment more than talent and reveals whether the vision is strong enough to withstand monotony and delay.

Visibility and Ownership

You step into what you have built. You claim your progress, share your work, and accept responsibility for outcomes. Visibility is not ego; it is accountability. You allow your efforts to be seen, evaluated, and refined, recognizing that ownership is a requirement of leadership and growth.

Reinvention and Expansion

Success does not conclude with achievement. It evolves. This phase involves reassessment and expansion—refining vision, stretching capacity, and avoiding stagnation through continual learning. Growth becomes a practice rather than a destination, ensuring that success remains dynamic rather than brittle.

Momentum, Reflection, and Growth

Sustained success is achieved through reflection and adjustment, not just intensity. Progress builds over small, consistent decisions made with awareness, even when progress feels irregular. Growth is rarely a straight line, and expecting it to be so often leads to unnecessary discouragement. What appears to be stagnation is often just integration occurring beneath the surface.

Setbacks and disruptions are unavoidable. What matters is not if life interrupts your progress, but whether you respond without losing yourself in the process. When the question shifts from "Why am I failing?" to "What must I learn here?", momentum stays intact. Reflection turns interruptions into lessons and helps prevent temporary setbacks from turning into permanent detours.

Success is influenced not only by circumstance but also by the responsibility you take for your response. Growth demands ownership—of decisions, perspective, and adjustment. When reflection becomes a practice rather than a reaction, progress remains possible even in uncertain or limited conditions.

Redefining Success from the Inside Out

Success is not something to be chased, captured, or proven. It is something built from the inside out—constructed through self-awareness, sustained through integrity, and expressed through lived alignment. When clarity deepens, strength follows. When perception shifts, possibility expands. The most durable forms of success do not arrive through force or urgency, but through coherence between who you are, what you value, and how you move through the world. External achievement may draw attention, but internal stability determines whether success can be held without fracture.

Forgiveness, clarity, and truth are not detours from success; they are its foundation. Without them, progress becomes brittle, and identity becomes performance. You cannot outgrow yourself, outrun unresolved patterns, or bypass inner alignment without cost. Growth is not an escape from who you are—it is an evolution with who you are. Success matures when ambition is informed by awareness and when striving is anchored in honesty rather than avoidance.

The Evolving Nature of Success

Over time, success reveals itself less through accumulation and more through transformation. The essential question shifts from "What did I gain?" to "Who did I become in the process?" Did you live with intention rather than reaction? Did you adapt when life required recalibration rather than resistance? Did you remain aligned with your values even as circumstances changed and certainty dissolved? These are the measures that endure when titles fade, and milestones lose their novelty.

The look of success will change as you do. What once represented arrival may later represent limitation. Learning to honor progress without clinging to form keeps success sustainable rather than confining. When success evolves alongside identity, it becomes expansive instead of exhausting. Each moment of clarity—each recalibration, each return to truth—does not signal an ending, but the quiet beginning of the next chapter.

Each chapter in this book will return to this moment—an invitation to pause, recalibrate, and choose with greater awareness.

THE SHIFT

Success rarely begins with certainty. It begins with permission.

Grant yourself permission to pause and reflect on whether the life you are creating truly belongs to you. Allow yourself to question inherited beliefs without shame. Recognize that what once motivated you may no longer suit the person you are becoming. This pause is not hesitation; it is discernment.

Most people measure success using borrowed standards. They follow timelines they did not create, pursue outcomes they did not consciously choose, and judge progress by criteria that do not align with their core values. The result is effort without fulfillment—movement without meaning.

Defining your personal idea of success is not an act of rebellion. It is a responsibility. When you clarify what truly matters to you now, your energy stops scattering. Focus sharpens. Choices become intentional. Success begins to provide structure rather than pressure.

This clarity does not remove struggle, nor does it promise ease. What it does is ensure that effort is directed toward what makes sense for your life, rather than toward meeting someone else's expectations. When you define success deliberately, progress becomes more sustainable. You stop proving yourself and start building.

The look of success is not revealed all at once. It is refined over time as awareness deepens. The willingness to revise your definition often signals genuine growth.

🕰 A Moment in Motion

The room is quiet except for the soft hum of a computer left on after hours. The workday has ended, but the questions remain. A list appears on the screen—goals once written with certainty now feel different. Some still resonate. Others feel heavy, outdated, or unexpectedly distant.

There is no crisis in the room. No dramatic loss. Only a growing awareness that achievement alone is no longer sufficient. In that stillness, a new understanding emerges: success does not require abandoning everything that has been built, but it may require redefining why it was built in the first place.

The screen goes dark.

The questions stay.

The Reflection

Before moving forward, pause here.
Not to evaluate progress.
Not to make a plan.
Simply to notice what is present.

Consider the questions below without urgency or judgment. Let them surface awareness rather than demand answers.

- How do you define success right now, and when was the last time you honestly reevaluated that definition?
- Which parts of your definition feel aligned with who you are now, and which parts feel inherited, assumed, or outdated?
- What external pressures—financial, cultural, relational, or social—are influencing your current goals?
- Where do you feel energized by your pursuit of success, and where do you feel depleted?
- If success had to be emotionally sustainable, what would need to change?

Success does not require certainty before action, but it does require awareness before commitment. The way you define success shapes how you spend your time, invest your energy, interpret setbacks, and measure progress. When that definition is unclear or misaligned, even meaningful accomplishments can feel hollow. When it is grounded and honest, effort begins to carry purpose.

There is no definitive answer to these questions. They are not meant to be resolved in a single sitting. They are meant to be revisited as your life evolves and your understanding deepens.

This chapter is not an ending. It is a recalibration.

Before moving on, carry this quiet understanding with you: success is not something you chase blindly. It is something you choose intentionally. And that choice begins with definition.

Capacity to Define

Before moving forward, hold this truth: success becomes sustainable only when it is defined from the inside out. Until you claim authorship over what success means in your life, effort will scatter and achievement will remain provisional—impressive perhaps, but fragile.

This chapter is not about arriving at certainty. It is about strengthening the capacity to define success deliberately rather than inheriting it unconsciously. When definition becomes intentional, progress gains direction. What follows is no longer driven by pressure or comparison, but by clarity.

CHAPTER TWO

TIME

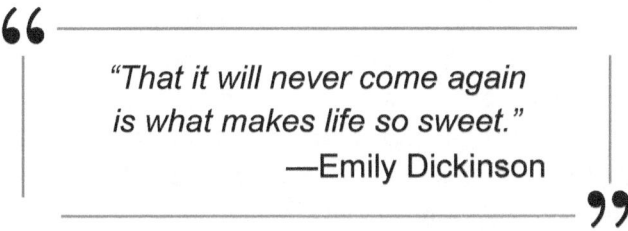

> "That it will never come again
> is what makes life so sweet."
> —Emily Dickinson

The Nature of Time

Everything takes time. Life itself is a process—unfolding moment by moment from beginning to end. No matter how carefully we plan or how urgently we desire results, time moves forward at its own pace. It does not negotiate. It does not pause. It does not reverse.

As we age, our perception of time changes. Childhood feels expansive, almost endless. Adulthood feels increasingly compressed. One year you are discovering who you are; the next, you are responsible for shaping outcomes that affect others. Time does not accelerate, but awareness deepens. You begin to recognize that moments are finite, seasons are temporary, and choices carry lasting weight.

One season you are imagining a future. Another season, you are living inside decisions you once only considered. A career ends unexpectedly. A relationship shifts. A parent grows older. A child leaves home. Someone you love dies. Time does not announce these transitions. It carries you into them quietly, often without permission.

Developing a Relationship With Time

Success requires more than ambition. It requires a relationship with time. Learning to work with time—rather than resist it—becomes essential. Time reveals patterns: when action is required, when patience is necessary, when persistence matters more than speed, and when release is the wiser choice.

Many people experience time as something to outrun or control. This posture creates anxiety, impatience, and exhaustion. Those who build sustainable success learn something different. Time responds to intention, discipline, and presence. When time is respected, it begins to support growth rather than undermine it.

Growth takes time. Learning takes time. Healing takes time. Grief takes time. Reinvention takes time. When expectations ignore these realities, frustration follows. When timelines are grounded in truth rather than urgency, progress becomes visible—even during periods that appear unproductive on the surface.

Flexibility and the Reality of Change

Time does not move in straight lines. Plans shift. Circumstances change. Life introduces interruptions that cannot be scheduled, predicted, or controlled.

A job loss can dismantle identity overnight. Retirement can remove structure before purpose has been fully redefined. Illness can slow the body while the mind races ahead. Divorce, caregiving, relocation, and grief create emotional terrain no calendar prepares you for. These moments place you in an in-between space—no longer who you were, not yet who you are becoming.

The instinct in these seasons is often to panic or rush, to replace what was lost as quickly as possible. But time does not respond well to fear. These seasons are not punishments. They are periods of repositioning. Something is ending so that something else can take form.

Flexibility becomes essential. Adaptation is not weakness; it is intelligence. When a plan no longer fits your reality, adjustment is not failure—it is maturity. Rigid thinking fractures under pressure. Flexible thinking evolves.

Time as Investment, Not Burden

Time feels heavy when effort lacks meaning. It feels lighter when purpose is present. This is why people can work tirelessly for what they believe in and feel depleted by tasks they merely endure. Purpose alters the experience of time. When energy aligns with intention, time becomes an investment rather than a burden.

Even in seasons of transition, time is not wasted. Reflection builds clarity. Stillness restores strength. Small, consistent actions accumulate quietly. Time rewards attention, multiplying whatever you commit to repeatedly—whether growth or avoidance, healing or stagnation.

Patience, Alignment, and Trust

Patience is not passivity. It is active alignment with timing. Some goals require immediate action; others require restraint. Wisdom lies in discerning the difference. Time often asks you to wait, not because you are incapable, but because conditions are still forming.

Waiting can feel especially uncomfortable when identity has been disrupted by loss or change. Yet many breakthroughs occur beneath the surface long before results appear. Trusting timing does not mean relinquishing responsibility. It means continuing to prepare while allowing life to unfold without force.

Choosing Yourself Through Time

Every person is moving toward something, whether consciously or by default. Even when intentions remain unspoken, time translates them into outcomes. Days accumulate into patterns, and patterns solidify into direction. Time is not neutral; it is the medium through which values are revealed and futures are shaped. What you consistently give your time to becomes the clearest expression of what you believe matters most.

Free will does not arrive as limitless opportunity. It arrives as twenty-four hours each day. Within that boundary lives choice. How you invest those hours determines not only what you build, but how you experience the process of becoming. When time is treated casually, life begins to feel reactive. When time is honored deliberately, life gains coherence. Direction emerges not from urgency, but from intention.

Rest is not a luxury within this equation; it is a requirement. Exhaustion distorts judgment, narrows perspective, and pushes capable people toward short-sighted decisions in the name of survival. Progress, too, requires space—not through dramatic leaps, but through consistent, repeatable actions that compound quietly over time. Reflection completes the cycle. Without it, patterns repeat unchecked, and growth stalls under the illusion of movement.

Choosing yourself does not mean withdrawing from others or abandoning responsibility. Selflessness is not self-erasure. True generosity begins with self-respect, because depleted people eventually give from resentment rather than clarity. When you honor your time, you honor your potential. You protect the conditions necessary for discernment, creativity, and resilience to take root.

Sustainable growth demands patience—an acceptance that meaningful transformation unfolds at the pace required for integrity, not comparison. Time will continue regardless of readiness or hesitation. The real question is not whether you have enough of it, but whether you are using it with intention. The look of success is built one choice at a time, measured not in urgency or productivity alone, but in alignment with who you are becoming.

THE SHIFT

Time is the most honest resource you possess.

It cannot be negotiated with, stored, or reclaimed. It moves at a constant pace, indifferent to intention, urgency, or regret. Yet the way you experience time is shaped entirely by how you choose to engage with it—not by how busy you are or how productive you appear, but by how deliberately you invest what passes through your hands each day.

Most people believe they are managing time when, in reality, time is managing them. Days fill quickly. Weeks blur. Life becomes reactive rather than intentional. In this state, success feels perpetually delayed—always scheduled for "later," when conditions improve or pressure eases.

But time does not reward delay. It responds to clarity.

When you understand what matters, time reorganizes itself. When you do not, it fragments. Attention scatters. Energy drains. The issue is rarely a lack of hours; it is a lack of alignment.

Time spent without intention creates motion without progress. Time invested with awareness builds momentum. The difference is not discipline alone, but choice—repeated quietly, consistently, and often unnoticed.

Learning to respect time is not about rushing. It is about recognizing that every commitment carries a cost. Every "yes" displaces something else. Every delay shapes a future version of your life.

Time will pass regardless. The question is whether it is shaping you, or whether you are shaping what it becomes.

🕐 A Moment in Motion

The calendar is full. Meetings stack back to back, messages wait unanswered, and the day moves forward without pause. Somewhere between obligations, a familiar thought surfaces: there should be more time than this—not because the hours are insufficient, but because so few of them feel fully lived. Time passes efficiently, yet something essential seems to slip through unnoticed.

Later that evening, the day returns in fragments. Not everything felt wasted, but not everything felt chosen either. A few moments stand out—brief, unplanned, unexpectedly grounding. They arrive without agenda and linger longer than the tasks that consumed most of the day. The rest feels compressed and hurried, blending together without distinction. Activity was constant, but presence was uneven.

Nothing catastrophic occurred. Nothing demands immediate correction or repair. And yet there is a quiet recognition that time was spent without being fully inhabited. The hours were filled, but not entirely held. This awareness does not accuse; it simply observes. It marks the difference between motion and meaning, between movement and intention.

Tomorrow will arrive regardless. Another schedule will form. Another series of choices will unfold. What remains open is not the promise of more time, but the possibility of entering it more fully.

The Reflection

Before moving forward, pause here.
Not to optimize your schedule.
Not to fix your habits.
Simply to observe how time is currently experienced.

Consider the questions below without judgment or urgency. Let them bring awareness, not correction.

- Where does your time go most consistently, and how intentional are those investments?
- Which parts of your day feel purposeful, and which feel reactive or fragmented?
- What responsibilities genuinely align with your values, and which persist out of obligation or momentum?
- Where do you feel rushed, and what belief is driving that urgency?
- If time were treated as a reflection of self-respect, what would need to change?

Time does not ask for perfection. It asks for awareness.

The way you use time reinforces what you believe is important. It shapes identity long before it produces visible results. When time is spent unconsciously, life begins to feel crowded and thin. When time is spent deliberately, even small windows carry weight.

You do not need more time to succeed. You need clearer standards for how time is used.

There is no single correct rhythm. Seasons differ. Demands fluctuate. What matters is not balance, but intention. Time aligned with values creates steadiness. Time spent in conflict with values creates exhaustion.

This chapter is not about controlling time. It is about reclaiming agency within it.

Before you move on, carry this understanding forward: time is not simply what passes. It is what you choose to honor. And success responds to what you honor consistently.

Capacity to Pace

Time does not respond to urgency; it responds to alignment. When time is treated as a resource to be stewarded rather than a force to be outrun, pressure begins to soften.

This chapter builds the capacity to pace success rather than rush toward it. Progress that honors rhythm endures longer than progress driven by urgency alone.

CHAPTER THREE

ENERGY

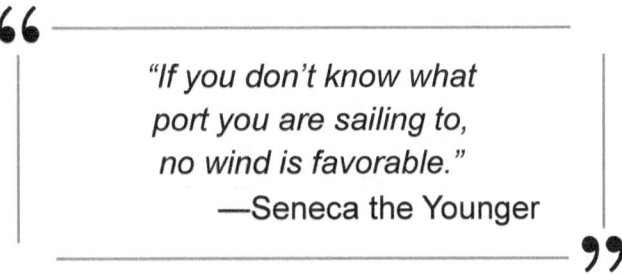

*"If you don't know what
port you are sailing to,
no wind is favorable."*
—Seneca the Younger

Energy as the Foundation of Movement

E verything operates on an energy plane. Movement, growth, and stability all depend on equilibrium. In human terms, equilibrium is the internal balance that allows you to move through changing circumstances without losing yourself. When balance is present, clarity follows. When it is disrupted, even simple decisions become difficult.

Extreme emotional states—whether excitement, grief, anger, or fear—distort perception. When perception is distorted, judgment weakens. You may feel busy but unproductive, motivated but unfocused, or driven yet disconnected from purpose. These experiences are not failures of discipline or willpower; they are indicators of energetic imbalance.

During periods of growth or transition, internal equilibrium often shifts before external conditions do. Many people experience this as restlessness, uncertainty, or emotional fatigue. Plans are started and abandoned. Focus scatters. Momentum slows. When energy is misaligned, progress in every area of life is affected, regardless of effort.

Balance Begins Internally

Restoring balance often requires returning inward before moving forward. Sometimes this means clarifying the direction you are moving toward. Other times it means tracing your steps backward to identify where alignment was lost. Even small internal adjustments can create movement across multiple areas of life. Energy responds quickly to honesty and intention.

As basic needs are met, attention naturally expands toward relationships, work, and purpose. When stability exists in these areas, energy flows outward with greater ease. When disruption enters— through loss, uncertainty, or prolonged stress—balance becomes harder to sustain. This is not a personal failure. It is a signal that restoration must begin internally before momentum can return.

Restoration and the Reality of Chaos

Restoration rarely begins in calm. It more often begins in confusion, pressure, or emotional overload. Order is rebuilt from disorder, not the other way around. Questions surface quietly or urgently: How do you regain stability after financial strain? How do you recover from a relationship that ended differently than you expected? How do you continue functioning when your environment no longer reflects your values?

There is rarely an immediate resolution. Restoration unfolds incrementally—one steady decision at a time. One boundary. One recalibration. Progress is subtle at first, often invisible, but it is real.

As stability returns in one area, energy begins to strengthen elsewhere. What once felt overwhelming becomes manageable. Clarity returns not through force, but through alignment. The work is not to eliminate chaos, but to restore enough internal balance to move through it without collapse.

The Power and Direction of Energy

Energy itself is neutral. What gives it direction is intention.

High energy anchored in clarity and care creates momentum that endures. High energy driven by resentment, fear, or ego may produce visible results, but those results are often unstable. Sustainable success requires energy that is aligned with purpose rather than reaction.

The look of success you experience is shaped by the energy you invest consistently. When effort is grounded in integrity, it sustains you. When it is driven by urgency alone, it eventually depletes you.

Pause and examine your current energy. Are you focused or fragmented? Engaged or exhausted? When momentum feels low, the question is rarely about what is missing externally. More often, it is about what requires attention internally.

Misused Energy and Self-Sabotage

Energy is often misdirected. Instead of being invested in growth, it is spent on comparison, self-doubt, resentment, or overexplaining yourself to people who are not aligned with your direction. These patterns do not usually announce themselves as self-sabotage. They feel justified, necessary, or unavoidable in the moment, even as they quietly erode momentum.

When internal imbalance exists, frustration is frequently projected outward—onto colleagues, partners, family members, or circumstances. Pain is externalized rather than examined. Energy that could support clarity or repair is instead consumed by reaction. Over time, this pattern delays resolution and reinforces the very conditions it seeks to escape.

Most people act from their level of awareness. What appears selfish, dismissive, or resistant is often rooted in unmet needs or limited perspective rather than intent. Interpreting every interaction as a personal offense drains energy that could be used for discernment, adjustment, or redirection. Awareness conserves energy. Assumption depletes it.

Success is influenced not only by action, but by interpretation. How you read the world shapes how you respond to it, and response determines where energy flows next.

Personality, Perspective, and Growth

Personality influences how energy is processed. Some people experience life holistically, recognizing patterns, relationships, and long-term consequences. Others approach challenges in fragments, addressing issues in isolation. Neither orientation is inherently flawed, but fragmentation without vision limits growth.

For example, viewing finances only as numbers rather than as part of a broader strategy can trap people in cycles of reaction rather than expansion. Perspective determines possibility. What you notice—and what you ignore—directs energy long before decisions are made.

Personality is not fixed. It evolves as awareness deepens. Patterns that once supported survival may no longer support expansion. As insight increases, energy recalibrates. Growth reshapes identity, and identity reshapes how energy is invested moving forward.

Alignment Over Effort

Effort alone does not create success. Alignment does.

Many people work hard while remaining internally divided. Habits go unchallenged. Comfort overrides clarity. Change is desired, but vulnerability is avoided. In these conditions, energy disperses. Action continues, but momentum stalls because effort is split between intention and resistance.

When commitment becomes whole—when effort is no longer fragmented—energy responds. What receives sustained, undivided attention begins to grow. Energy mirrors honesty. What you invest in repeatedly becomes reinforced, whether that investment is conscious or not.

Not every environment supports growth. Misaligned relationships drain energy regardless of intention. Talent dulls under constant tension. Even strong effort loses effectiveness when it is spent compensating for misfit rather than building toward purpose. Growth requires compatibility between vision and environment. Alignment is not about perfection; it is about coherence.

Visibility, Responsibility, and Choice

Energy is visible long before it is consciously acknowledged. Stress, vitality, confidence, and depletion leave traces that accumulate over time, shaping how a person moves, speaks, and engages with the world. External presentation may amplify presence, but it cannot compensate for unresolved inner imbalance. Eventually, what is carried internally announces itself externally—not through a single moment, but through patterns that become increasingly difficult to ignore.

Responsibility for energy cannot be outsourced. Feeling stuck is rarely random or sudden; it is more often the result of repeated choices made without reflection, boundaries, or recalibration. Small compromises accumulate. Unexamined habits harden into routine. Over time, momentum slows not because capacity has diminished, but because alignment has eroded. The good news is that no condition is permanent. Awareness restores agency, and agency creates the conditions for change.

Change remains available at every stage, but it is not passive. It requires honesty about what is no longer working, discipline to interrupt familiar patterns, and internal effort that extends beyond surface-level adjustment. Transformation does not begin with force or urgency. It begins with clarity. When clarity is present, direction follows.

Energy as the Engine of Success

The look of success is sustained by energy long before it is reflected in outcomes. Progress depends on alignment—between intention and action, values and environment, effort and recovery.

Circumstances will inevitably change, but a clearly held vision has the capacity to evolve rather than collapse under pressure. When energy is directed with intention, success becomes sustainable rather than exhausting.

When something feels stalled or fragmented, the most effective response is inward evaluation. Which habits are quietly draining vitality? Which commitments no longer align with who you are becoming? Which environments scatter focus rather than support depth? These questions are not meant to judge; they are meant to refine. Awareness sharpens choice.

Scattered energy produces shallow results. Aligned energy produces depth, coherence, and longevity. Disorder in one area of life rarely remains contained; it spills outward, disrupting focus elsewhere. Dishonesty with self—through avoidance, overcommitment, or denial—leads to stagnation. Time begins to feel lost. Momentum fades not from lack of effort, but from misdirected effort.

At times, the remedy is distance. Stepping away from noise, routine, or familiar patterns creates the space necessary for recalibration. Pause restores direction. Reflection renews clarity. When energy is gathered rather than dispersed, movement becomes intentional again, and success resumes its natural rhythm.

Energy, Intention, and Sustainability

Energy, intention, and alignment determine not only whether goals are reached, but whether they can be sustained once achieved. Momentum without clarity eventually collapses under its own weight. Progress driven solely by pressure or external validation may produce visible results, but it often does so at the expense of stability. When alignment is absent, success becomes something that must be defended rather than lived.

Success built without alignment always carries a cost. It shows up as exhaustion, fragmentation, or the quiet realization that achievement has outpaced fulfillment. In contrast, success built with clarity creates longevity. It allows growth to expand without eroding identity. When intention guides effort and values inform direction, progress no longer feels adversarial. It becomes integrated—something that strengthens rather than depletes.

Energy is not incidental to this process; it is foundational. It fuels decision-making, shapes resilience, and determines how consistently effort can be sustained over time. Your energy is the engine behind everything you build. When it is protected, directed, and renewed with intention, success stops requiring constant recovery and becomes something you can inhabit. Alignment does not slow progress—it makes it survivable.

THE SHIFT

Energy is not infinite, and it is not neutral.

It rises and falls based on how you live, what you tolerate, and what you repeatedly ignore. While time moves forward regardless of choice, energy responds immediately to alignment—or the absence of it. You can have hours available and still feel depleted. You can have limited time and still feel steady, focused, and capable. The difference is energy management, not effort.

Most people attempt to succeed by pushing harder rather than listening more closely. They override fatigue. They normalize depletion. They mistake endurance for strength. Over time, this approach erodes clarity and dulls motivation. Progress slows not because of laziness, but because energy has been misallocated.

Energy is shaped by more than rest. It is influenced by emotional labor, unresolved tension, unspoken resentment, constant comparison, and environments that demand performance without restoration. When these drains go unexamined, even meaningful goals begin to feel heavy.

Sustainable success requires discernment. Not every opportunity deserves your energy. Not every demand warrants compliance. When energy is invested without intention, burnout follows. When it is invested with awareness, momentum becomes possible again.

Energy does not ask for perfection.

It asks for honesty.

Learning to protect and direct your energy is not self-indulgence. It is responsibility. You cannot build a meaningful life while consistently draining the very force that allows you to show up within it.

⏱ A Moment in Motion

The task itself is simple. Familiar. Something done dozens of times before. Yet today, resistance lingers. Focus slips. The body feels heavier than expected. There is no clear reason—no illness, no obvious stressor—just a quiet depletion that makes even small efforts feel costly.

Later, in a rare pause, the pattern becomes clearer. Too many conversations required restraint. Too many obligations demanded presence without permission to disengage. Energy was spent long before the task began.

Nothing dramatic happened.

But something essential was overextended.

The Reflection

Before moving forward, pause here.
Not to push through fatigue.
Not to motivate yourself.
Simply to notice how energy is currently experienced.

- What activities, environments, or interactions consistently energize you?
- What drains your energy most predictably, even when those drains appear productive or necessary?
- Where are you expending emotional energy without acknowledgment or recovery?
- What signals does your body give when your energy is mis-aligned—and how often do you ignore them?
- If energy were treated as a finite investment, what would you need to protect more carefully?

Energy does not disappear randomly. It follows patterns.

The way you manage energy shapes how you experience effort, resilience, and satisfaction. When energy is respected, challenges feel workable. When it is neglected, even success feels exhausting.

You do not need to eliminate effort to preserve energy. You need to align effort with purpose. Energy spent in alignment restores itself more readily. Energy spent in contradiction accumulates strain.

There is no ideal level of energy to maintain at all times. Life requires exertion. What matters is recovery, awareness, and choice. When energy is repeatedly drained without replenishment, success becomes unsustainable—even when goals are achieved.

This chapter is not about doing less.

It is about doing what matters with integrity.

Before you move on, carry this understanding forward: energy is not something to consume recklessly. It is something to steward deliberately.

And success depends on how well you protect what fuels it.

⸻ ◆ ⸻

Capacity to Regulate

Energy is not infinite, and success that ignores this truth eventually becomes extractive. What matters is not how much energy you expend, but how consciously you choose where it goes.

This chapter strengthens the capacity to regulate energy so effort remains intentional rather than reactive. When energy is directed with awareness, success no longer competes with well-being.

CHAPTER FOUR

DETERMINATION

> " *"I have striven not to laugh at human actions, not to weep at them, nor to hate them, but to understand them."*
> —Benedict Spinoza "

Determination Begins With Focus

When people pursue a goal, they often believe what they need most is willpower. In moments of difficulty, they search for strength as though it must be summoned from somewhere outside themselves. In reality, determination begins with focus. And within focus, courage and strength are formed, refined, and reinforced.

This becomes especially clear during periods of disruption—after job loss, forced career change, retirement, illness, or personal loss. In those moments, motivation may feel absent. Confidence may waver. But determination does not require certainty. It requires direction.

When the mind fixes itself on a goal—even a modest one—momentum follows. Focused energy creates movement. Direction, not intensity, determines outcome.

Focus as a Force Multiplier

A focused mind leaves little room for distraction. Determination is sustained by mental posture. The thoughts you return to repeatedly shape the actions you take, and over time, those actions shape your reality.

When internal dialogue is rooted in clarity, responsibility, and possibility, energy stabilizes. When thinking remains anchored in loss, comparison, or delay, progress slows. Inconsistent self-talk produces inconsistent results.

Many people abandon focus prematurely because they expect immediate transformation. Determination, however, is cumulative. Small, consistent shifts in focus—maintained over time—can redirect an entire trajectory.

The Discipline of Prioritization

Focus cannot be scattered. Success requires prioritization. You cannot fully commit to everything at once. At any given moment, one area must receive primary attention—health, financial stability, emotional recovery, skill development, or rebuilding professional identity.

This raises an uncomfortable but necessary question: *can success coexist with balance?*

For some, balance is achievable. For many, balance is seasonal rather than constant. Certain chapters of life require concentrated effort. Determination demands sacrifice, but sacrifice does not require suffering. Society does not get to dictate your priorities. Only you can determine what deserves your focus *now.*

Determination Is Not Accidental

Success is never accidental. Even those born into advantage must apply sustained focus to maintain or expand what they have. Opportunity may open doors, but determination determines whether anything meaningful is built beyond the threshold.

Determination is not inherited, nor does it appear fully formed. It is practiced—shaped through repeated choices, disciplined attention, and the willingness to remain engaged when ease gives way to effort.

When focus is self-generated rather than externally imposed, alignment follows. Energy sharpens. Action becomes consistent rather than episodic. Determination shifts from reactive to deliberate, no longer dependent on pressure, praise, or circumstance. What once required force begins to feel natural, because effort is now anchored in intention rather than urgency.

Willpower cannot be performed or declared. It is revealed quietly through behavior over time. Words may express intention, but action exposes commitment. When language and behavior conflict, action tells the truth every time. Determination lives not in what is promised, but in what is repeatedly chosen.

Clarity Creates Willpower

Determination strengthens as clarity increases. Goals that are defined, revisited, and refined provide direction, especially during seasons of transition. Without vision, movement scatters and progress loses coherence. Some goals require structure and precision. Others require adaptability and openness. Most are not final destinations at all, but stepping stones—necessary phases within a longer unfolding.

The process does not conclude; it evolves. Achievement does not signal completion, but recalibration. Fulfillment is often found not after a goal is reached, but within the act of pursuing something meaningful. When effort is connected to purpose, creativity expands and endurance deepens. Purpose sustains determination long after motivation fades, allowing progress to continue with steadiness rather than strain.

Growth Expands Responsibility

Transformation rarely concludes with a single milestone. More often, a milestone marks the beginning of a new phase of responsibility. Each level of growth introduces greater complexity and calls for deeper awareness, stronger discipline, and increased ownership. What once required effort now requires stewardship. Expansion demands not only ambition, but the capacity to preserve what has been built without distortion.

Gratitude plays a stabilizing role in this process. It grounds perspective and prevents growth from hardening into entitlement or exhaustion. When difficulty is reframed as instruction, progress becomes less adversarial and more intentional. At times, movement does not require additional effort at all—it requires clearer interpretation. Understanding what a moment is asking of you often enables more effective action than force.

Identity, Vision, and Ownership

Understanding who you are becoming—and why—remains essential as growth unfolds. Many people wait for external validation before claiming a new identity, believing permission must precede embodiment. Yet external approval can never define internal direction. Identity matures when it is assumed with intention rather than granted by circumstance.

Confidence, in this context, must be internally generated. When self-image depends on others' perception, determination weakens under scrutiny. When vision is outsourced, alignment collapses. Ownership restores coherence. Determination is not sustained by reassurance, but by responsibility—the willingness to stand inside a chosen direction even when affirmation is absent.

The Inevitability of Aligned Success

True determination is not forceful or frantic. It is coherent. It emerges through alignment—of focus with clarity, responsibility with intention, effort with understanding. When direction is clear, excess strain disappears.

When determination is rooted in understanding rather than pressure, success becomes sustainable. It no longer rises and falls with circumstance or approval. It stabilizes. Over time, aligned success does not need to be chased or defended. It becomes inevitable.

THE SHIFT

Determination is often misunderstood.

It is not intensity, nor is it constant motivation. It is not the absence of doubt or fatigue. Determination is the decision to continue in the presence of both. It is steadiness, not force.

Many people confuse determination with pressure. They believe that if they stop pushing, progress will stall. As a result, they rely on urgency, self-criticism, or fear of failure to maintain momentum. This approach may yield short-term results, but it erodes self-trust over time.

True determination is quieter. It is built on commitment rather than emotion. It does not require enthusiasm to function. It operates through clarity and choice—returning repeatedly to what matters, even when conditions are imperfect.

Determination grows when purpose is clear. When goals are misaligned, determination weakens—not because of a lack of will, but because the cost no longer makes sense. When goals are honest, determination stabilizes effort rather than exhausting it.

Determination is not about never wavering.

It is about recommitting without drama when wavering occurs.

🕰 A Moment in Motion

The decision was made weeks ago. The plan was outlined. The first steps were taken with confidence. Then life intervened—not dramatically, just enough to disrupt rhythm. Momentum slowed. Doubt crept in quietly.

There is a pause before the next action. Not because the goal no longer matters, but because resistance has arrived. Fatigue. Distraction. Competing priorities. In that pause, a choice waits to be made—not whether to feel ready, but whether to continue without certainty.

The work resumes.

Not perfectly.

Not quickly.

Just steadily.

The Reflection

Before moving forward, pause here.
Not to recommit loudly.
Not to push yourself harder.
Simply examine how determination currently operates in your life.

- What commitments have you sustained over time, even when motivation faded?
- Where do you rely on pressure or urgency to stay consistent?

- What goals feel worth continuing even when progress is slow or invisible?
- Where have you mistaken exhaustion for a lack of determination?
- If determination were defined as steadiness rather than force, what would change?

Determination does not require constant intensity. It requires trust.

The way you relate to difficulty determines whether determination becomes resilience or rigidity. When you allow yourself to adapt without quitting, determination strengthens. When you demand perfection, it fractures.

Determination is reinforced through follow-through, not self-punishment. Each time you return to your intention without self-betrayal, you build credibility with yourself. Over time, that credibility becomes one of your most reliable strengths.

This chapter is not about pushing through at all costs.

It is about staying engaged without abandoning yourself.

Before you move on, carry this understanding forward: determination is not proven by how hard you push, but by how consistently you return.

And success responds to those who keep returning.

Capacity to Persist Without Hardening

Determination is often misunderstood as force. In reality, it is sustained responsiveness—the ability to continue without becoming rigid, bitter, or closed.

This chapter refines the capacity to persist without hardening. Success that remains flexible under pressure preserves both progress and perspective.

CHAPTER FIVE

ACTION

> "Twenty years from now, you will be more disappointed by the things that you didn't do than by the ones you did do. So throw off the bowlines. Sail away from the safe harbor. Catch the trade winds in your sails. Explore. Dream. Discover."
>
> —Mark Twain

Action Gives Success Its Shape

The look of success only takes form through action. Action is the point at which intention becomes embodied. Vision without action remains conceptual—capable of insight, but incapable of transformation. Action gives success structure. It translates thought into direction and potential into movement.

Action does not require certainty. It requires engagement. Each step taken—whether deliberate or experimental—creates information. Action builds a living plan, revealing what works, what resists, and what needs recalibration. Detours are not evidence of failure; they are often the experiences that clarify direction and deepen discernment.

During periods of transition—after job loss, relocation, retirement, or personal upheaval—action restores agency. It counters paralysis and reminds you that while circumstances may change, the capacity to choose movement remains intact. Action does not erase uncertainty, but it prevents stagnation from becoming identity.

Action as a Dialogue With Life

Life does not respond to action in predictable ways. Sometimes it reinforces direction. Sometimes it redirects entirely. When approached with awareness rather than rigidity, these responses become information rather than obstruction.

Action does not guarantee outcomes. It generates feedback. And feedback—when interpreted honestly—is how growth accelerates.

At times, what you believe will move you forward may reveal unseen resistance. Frustration often follows. But resistance is not proof of error; it is an invitation to refine approach, timing, or scope. Progress requires discernment: the ability to move decisively without becoming inflexible, to act without demanding immediate confirmation.

Action is not about forcing results. It is about movement, observation, learning, and adjustment. Without action, potential remains dormant. The goals and ideas that persist within you do so not to be protected indefinitely, but to be tested, shaped, and strengthened through experience.

Starting Where You Are

There is no ideal moment to begin. Waiting for perfect conditions often delays progress indefinitely, not because readiness never arrives, but because certainty is mistaken for permission. Momentum begins when you work with what is available rather than postponing action until circumstances feel complete.

Constraints do not eliminate action; they shape it. Limited resources sharpen judgment. Limited clarity invites experimentation. Limited confidence is strengthened through repetition rather than reassurance. Action adapts to reality—it does not require perfection to function.

If knowledge is lacking, learning becomes the action.

If confidence is low, consistency becomes the action.

If direction is unclear, movement provides feedback.

Progress does not begin where conditions are optimal. It begins where awareness meets choice.

Support Without Dependency

Action does not require isolation. Mentors, advisors, coaches, and collaborators can provide perspective, reduce error, and expand possibilities. Thoughtful guidance shortens learning curves and prevents unnecessary repetition of mistakes.

However, support is not a substitute for ownership. Responsibility for direction cannot be delegated. Others may advise, challenge, or accompany you—but they cannot choose movement on your behalf. Action must be initiated, sustained, and recalibrated by the individual pursuing the vision.

Support can accelerate momentum.

Ownership is what sustains it.

Flexibility Over Force

Sustainable action is adaptive. Rigid effort often breaks under pressure, while flexible action adjusts to changing conditions without losing direction. Progress rarely follows a straight line, and expecting it to do so often leads to unnecessary frustration.

What worked in one season may require revision in the next. Circumstances shift, capacity changes, and insight deepens over time. Effective action responds to reality rather than clinging to outdated strategies.

Effective action listens to results. Feedback informs direction and prevents wasted effort. Discipline is not blind repetition; it is committed awareness that remains responsive to what action reveals.

Growth often feels uncomfortable not because it is wrong, but because it is unfamiliar. Discomfort is frequently a signal of expansion rather than error. Learning to tolerate that discomfort without forcing outcomes is part of sustainable progress.

What appears as failure may actually be refinement. What feels like delay may be preparation taking place beneath the surface. Action reveals what reflection alone cannot by exposing assumptions, limits, and hidden strengths.

Consistency and Transformation

Consistent action produces development over time. Skills sharpen through repetition, confidence builds through experience, and perspective widens as understanding deepens. Progress that appears gradual on the surface often produces lasting internal change.

Over time, sustained effort reshapes identity—not through declaration, but through practice. You become what you repeatedly choose to do, especially when no one is watching. Identity evolves as behavior aligns more closely with intention.

As growth occurs, some relationships strengthen while others naturally fall away. This is not loss, but alignment taking shape. Action clarifies which connections support your direction and which belong to earlier chapters.

Periods of rest and reflection are essential to this process. Stillness is not abandonment; it is recalibration that prevents burnout and distortion. Action and pause operate together to sustain long-term momentum and preserve clarity.

Belief as the Engine of Action

Action is sustained by belief long before results become visible. When outcomes feel distant or uncertain, belief bridges the gap between effort and patience. Motivation fluctuates with circumstance, but belief anchors consistency by providing quiet assurance that progress is unfolding even when evidence is incomplete.

Without belief, action becomes sporadic and reactive. Effort fragments when it is driven only by mood or short-term reinforcement. With belief in place, action gains rhythm and direction, allowing consistency to form even in the absence of immediate reward.

Understanding *why* you move toward something matters more than how quickly you move. Purpose fuels endurance by giving effort meaning beyond visible progress. When intention is clear, action becomes deliberate rather than draining, and persistence feels grounded rather than forced.

Clarity has a stabilizing effect that extends beyond the individual. When effort is coherent, energy accumulates rather than disperses. Others respond to that coherence, reinforcing momentum and allowing progress to sustain itself over time.

Ownership and Alignment

Responsibility for success ultimately rests with the individual. Assistance may appear in the form of opportunity, mentorship, or support, but ownership itself cannot be delegated. Progress becomes unstable when responsibility is externalized rather than claimed.

Clarity about what you offer—your skills, insight, value, and effort—strengthens both direction and confidence. When contribution is understood internally rather than asserted outwardly, action becomes steadier. Self-trust deepens because movement is rooted in alignment rather than validation.

Preparation and timing matter, but alignment matters most. What is meant for you cannot be forced into existence through urgency alone. Progress driven by impatience often collapses under its own pressure, while aligned action endures.

When action aligns with values, intention, and purpose, life responds—not always immediately, but meaningfully. Results emerge in forms that support sustainability rather than momentary validation. Alignment does not eliminate challenge, but it ensures effort contributes to growth rather than depletion.

Action as Commitment

Action is not a single decision or dramatic turning point; it is a practice sustained over time. Each step reinforces commitment. Each adjustment sharpens discernment. Each effort clarifies direction. Through action, belief becomes behavior and intention becomes lived experience.

Importance is not defined by declaration, but by embodiment. You choose how to invest your energy, where to apply focus, and what to protect over time. When action is taken with clarity, discipline, and alignment, success moves beyond possibility and becomes durable. It becomes something that can be carried forward without erosion of purpose, identity, or self-respect.

THE SHIFT

Action is where intention becomes visible.

It is the point at which clarity, time, energy, and determination move from internal agreement into external reality. Without action, even the most thoughtful plans remain theoretical. Yet action, when disconnected from purpose, quickly becomes motion without meaning.

Many people delay action while waiting to feel ready. They seek certainty, confidence, or ideal conditions before proceeding. But readiness is not a prerequisite for action; it is often the result of it.

Action clarifies what thinking alone cannot. It exposes gaps, reveals resistance, and refines direction. Through action, assumptions are tested, feedback appears, and learning accelerates. Progress becomes measurable—not because outcomes are guaranteed, but because movement has begun.

Effective action is not impulsive. It is intentional. It does not require urgency to be productive; it requires commitment to small, repeatable steps that align with a larger vision. When action is consistent, confidence follows naturally.

Action is not about doing more.

It is about doing what matters—again and again—until momentum replaces hesitation.

⏱ A Moment in Motion

The list has been rewritten multiple times. The ideas are clear. The plan is sound. Still, there is hesitation before the first visible step. Not fear exactly—more a quiet resistance to being seen in the early stages.

Eventually, the decision is made to begin without refinement. The first action is imperfect. Slightly uncomfortable. Surprisingly grounding. What once felt overwhelming now feels manageable.

Nothing dramatic has changed.

But something shifts internally.

Movement replaces anticipation. Progress replaces speculation.

The work is no longer hypothetical.

The Reflection

Before moving forward, pause here.
Not to expand your goals.
Not to accelerate your pace.
Simply observe your relationship with action.

- Where do you tend to overthink instead of act?
- What small actions have you delayed while waiting for certainty or confidence?
- Which actions align most clearly with the success you want to build?
- Where does fear of imperfection slow your momentum?
- If action were measured by consistency rather than scale, what would you begin today?

Action does not require boldness to be effective. It requires presence and willingness. When action is approached as engagement rather than performance, pressure decreases and clarity becomes more accessible.

Each step taken creates information. Each attempt refines direction and exposes what thinking alone cannot resolve. When action is avoided, uncertainty grows. When action is engaged, clarity follows—even when outcomes differ from expectation.

You do not need to act perfectly to succeed. You need to act honestly and remain responsive to what action reveals. Progress favors those willing to learn while moving rather than those who remain stalled in preparation.

This chapter is not about speed. It is about follow-through over time. Consistency, not urgency, is what allows momentum to take hold.

Before you move on, carry this understanding forward: action is not the result of confidence—it is the source of it. Confidence accumulates through engagement, not contemplation. And success responds to those who begin.

Capacity to Act Without Overattachment

Action gives form to intention, but action driven by urgency can distort direction. When movement becomes performative, momentum replaces meaning, and outcomes begin to matter more than alignment. In these conditions, effort accelerates while discernment quietly erodes.

This chapter develops the capacity to act with commitment rather than overattachment. Action grounded in clarity allows success to unfold without being consumed by outcome or external validation. When engagement remains intentional, progress stays responsive, resilient, and sustainable over time.

CHAPTER SIX

WANTING SUCCESS

> " *"To live content with small means; to seek elegance rather than luxury, and refinement rather than fashion; to be worthy, not respectable, and wealthy, not rich; to study hard, think quietly, talk gently, act frankly; to listen to stars and birds, to babes and sages, with open heart; to bear all cheerfully, do all bravely, await occasions, hurry never. In a word, to let the spiritual, unbidden, and unconscious grow up through the common. This is to be my symphony."*
> —William Henry Channing "

Desire as the Starting Point

To achieve success, you must start with a dream—not just a vague wish or fleeting thought. It needs to be a clear vision you're willing to chase, even when circumstances are tough and support is lacking. Wanting success isn't passive; it's an active pursuit that demands ownership, discipline, and persistence.

Some people wait for success to arrive through recognition, opportunity, or permission. They believe that wanting is sufficient, assuming that momentum will follow desire automatically. But desire alone does not produce movement; it must be accompanied by willingness to act without guarantees.

Wanting success means embracing uncertainty as part of the journey. It requires pushing ahead before validation shows and persevering even when progress is slow or invisible. Desire becomes meaningful only when paired with responsibility.

Wanting Versus Depending

Many successful people speak of mentors, guidance, or strong support systems. While mentorship can accelerate growth, it is not a prerequisite for success. Waiting to be guided can quietly become a reason for delay rather than a strategy for development.

Sometimes growth occurs in solitude. When external guidance is unavailable, internal discipline becomes essential. Learning how to seek knowledge independently—through study, reflection, experimentation, and risk-taking—builds resilience and strengthens self-trust over time.

Mentorship is a gift, not an entitlement. Support cannot replace initiative, and direction cannot substitute for ownership. Until internal alignment is established, self-leadership remains the foundation on which success is built.

Alignment Before Assistance

Wanting success requires learning how to listen—especially when direction arrives quietly. Insight often emerges through reflection, curiosity, reading, observation, and moments of clarity that cannot be forced. Guidance rarely announces itself loudly, and it is often missed when attention is scattered or rushed.

When alignment exists, information begins to surface naturally. What you need finds you when you remain open to learning rather than fixated on control. Assistance becomes useful only after clarity has been established.

Support follows alignment, not the other way around. When desire is disciplined, and intention is clear, help appears as reinforcement rather than rescue. Wishing for success, at its highest level, means being prepared to accept assistance without becoming dependent on it.

Success as an Internal State

Many people pursue success as something external, believing it resides in titles, possessions, or recognition. Yet success begins internally, long before it becomes visible. It is rooted in wholeness, presence, and integrity—the quiet coherence between values, intention, and action. External markers may follow this internal alignment, but they do not define fulfillment. Without inner stability, even the most visible achievements remain fragile.

When success is pursued primarily for validation, it rarely satisfies. Accomplishments earned to prove worth often create temporary elevation followed by a deeper sense of emptiness. Applause fades, standards shift, and the cycle begins again. Fulfillment emerges not from being seen, but from being aligned. Purpose—not recognition—determines whether success can be inhabited without erosion of self.

Purpose Sustains Desire

Desiring success requires clarity about *why* it matters. Purpose gives ambition direction and endurance, allowing effort to remain steady when momentum slows. Without purpose, ambition fragments—chasing outcomes that never fully resolve. With purpose, effort gains meaning, and persistence becomes sustainable rather than exhausting.

Timing influences opportunity, but timing is not luck. It is alignment meeting readiness. Preparation intersects with awareness, and awareness sharpens discernment. Success is not accidental, yet it remains responsive—unfolding as internal growth catches up with external possibility.

We are not here by chance. Abilities, inclinations, and insight are not incidental or misplaced. Faith, in this context, is the willingness to continue forward even when the path is incomplete, while remaining open to refinement as conditions evolve. When purpose is honored internally, success no longer needs to be chased. It reveals itself through alignment, patience, and trust in the process of becoming.

Growth Requires Evolution

Success does not reward complacency. Growth demands adaptation, awareness, and the willingness to evolve as conditions change. When individuals or organizations stop evolving, progress slows, and comfort quietly becomes a liability. What once felt stabilizing can begin to restrict movement—not because growth is no longer possible, but because familiarity has replaced intentional expansion.

At times, stagnation is not the result of insufficient effort, but of environmental misalignment. People, systems, or values that no longer resonate can drain energy and dull clarity over time. Remaining aligned—even when it requires change—creates space for opportunities that are more congruent to emerge. Evolution is not a betrayal of what once worked; it is a disciplined response to what is now required.

Authentic Desire Cannot Be Imitated

Desire cannot be manufactured, and alignment cannot be performed. Wanting success requires honesty—about what you are willing to work for, what you are prepared to protect, and who you are willing to grow into. Without this honesty, effort becomes performative, and progress remains shallow. Action may be visible, but direction remains unstable.

Curiosity strengthens desire by sustaining engagement over time. Questions deepen understanding, and clarity sharpens focus. Success pursued for surface-level reasons fades quickly because it lacks the internal structure to withstand resistance. In contrast, success rooted in purpose develops resilience. It is sustained not by excitement alone, but by meaning that persists long after novelty fades.

Persistence matters. Consistency matters. Belief matters. External support may arrive later—or not at all—but internal coherence must be established first. Without a stable internal ecosystem, no amount of validation can stabilize progress for long.

Owning Your Evolution

As growth unfolds, not everyone will recognize who you are becoming. Some will continue to relate to a version of you that no longer exists. That disconnect does not require explanation, justification, or correction. Familiarity is not an obligation.

Truth does not need defense. Growth does not require permission. Alignment communicates itself through action, posture, and choice. Wanting success is not about convincing others of your worth; it is about choosing environments—physical, relational, and energetic—that support expansion rather than resist it. Ownership of evolution is not loud or confrontational. It is quiet, deliberate, and unwavering.

Guarding What You Want to Build

What you are building requires protection. Vision is fragile in its early stages—not because it is weak, but because it is still forming. Guarding your energy, being deliberate with your time, and choosing where to place your effort are acts of responsibility rather than defensiveness. Not every audience deserves access to your process. Do not exhaust yourself attempting to prove your direction to those who are committed to misunderstanding it. Consistency will always communicate more powerfully than explanation.

Goals thrive in environments that nourish them. Just as growth in nature depends on the right conditions, meaningful progress requires context—people, rhythms, values, and systems that support expansion rather than erode it. Intentional care matters. Vision strengthens when it is fed with clarity and protected from unnecessary exposure. Much of what eventually becomes visible is first cultivated quietly, away from noise, comparison, and premature scrutiny.

Success begins with wanting it deeply—not as fantasy or entitlement, but as responsibility. It asks for stewardship, discipline, and alignment between belief and behavior. You were not created to merely imagine success, but to carry it with integrity. What sustains success is not constant striving, but the decision to live as though what you are building already exists within you—expressed through how you choose, how you prepare, and how you show up long before results are visible.

THE SHIFT

Wanting success is often treated as something to outgrow. People are encouraged to be practical, realistic, or grateful for what they already have—as though desire itself were a flaw to manage rather than a signal to understand. Over time, wanting becomes muted, rationalized, or dismissed altogether. Yet wanting is not weakness. It is information.

Desire reveals direction before strategy exists. It points toward unmet needs, unrealized potential, and values that have not yet found expression. When wanting is ignored, ambition dulls and momentum weakens. When examined honestly, clarity begins to take shape.

Wanting success does not mean craving validation or excess. It means acknowledging that something within you is reaching forward. That reach deserves attention—not indulgence, but respect. Desire without discipline creates restlessness. Discipline without desire creates emptiness. Sustainable success requires the integration of both.

Many people suppress wanting because they fear disappointment. Others confuse wanting with entitlement and feel obligated to minimize it. But wanting, when paired with responsibility, becomes stabilizing rather than destabilizing. It provides the emotional fuel that makes effort coherent and commitment meaningful.

Wanting is not the opposite of contentment.

It is the beginning of intention.

⏱ A Moment in Motion

The thought arrives unexpectedly—during a quiet moment, not in the middle of planning. A simple realization surfaces: I want more than this. Not more in excess. More in alignment. More room to grow. More honesty in how life is lived.

The thought lingers. It would be easy to dismiss it as unrealistic or inconvenient. Responsibilities exist. Commitments are real. Still, the desire does not disappear. It waits—steady, persistent, unresolved.

Nothing changes immediately. But the wanting has been acknowledged. And that acknowledgment subtly alters how the future is imagined.

The Reflection

Before moving forward, pause here.
Not to justify your desire.
Not to minimize it.
Simply to understand it.

- What does success mean to you right now—not what it *should* mean, but what it actually means?
- What do you want that you have been hesitant to name clearly?
- Where have you dismissed desire in favor of practicality or expectation?
- What fears surface when you allow yourself to want more?
- If wanting were treated as a form of self-awareness rather than indulgence, what would you listen to differently?

Wanting does not obligate you to immediate action. It invites honesty.

The desires you carry influence how you interpret opportunity, risk, and effort. When wanting is suppressed, motivation fades. When it is clarified, energy begins to organize itself around purpose. Wanting gives direction to time, focus to action, and meaning to persistence.

Not every desire must be pursued. But every desire deserves to be understood. Discernment begins with acknowledgment, not denial.

This chapter is not about longing endlessly. It is about recognizing that wanting is often the first signal of change—the emotional cue that something new is possible, even when the path forward is not yet clear.

Before you move on, carry this understanding forward: wanting success is not a flaw to overcome. It is a signal to pay attention.

And success begins where desire is taken seriously.

Capacity to Desire Honestly

Wanting success is not the problem. Distorted desire is. When wanting is shaped by comparison, urgency, or unexamined expectation, it loses clarity and direction.

This chapter strengthens the capacity to desire success honestly—without minimizing ambition or inflating it through external pressure. Clear desire becomes a stabilizing force rather than a restless one.

CHAPTER SEVEN

HAVING SUCCESS

> 66
>
> *"The greater part of our happiness or misery depends upon our dispositions, and not upon our circumstances."*
> —Martha Washington
>
> 99

Recognizing Success Where You Are

Having success means different things to different people. Often, it is defined by reaching a place that once felt distant—financial stability, professional achievement, academic accomplishment, meaningful relationships, or a life shaped by choice rather than survival. Success exists in the goals we set and the milestones we cross, but it gains meaning only through perception.

You define what success looks like. Your interpretation gives it weight. Frequently, success exists closer than we realize—sometimes already present but unacknowledged. Comparison complicates this recognition. You may still experience yourself as striving while others already view you as successful.

If success is always imagined as something ahead of you, it will never fully register when it arrives. Part of having success is recognizing it, owning it, and allowing yourself to experience it without immediately moving the goalpost.

Success Beyond Symbols

Many people attempt to validate success through external markers—titles, possessions, visibility, or lifestyle. While these symbols may reflect achievement, they do not guarantee fulfillment. When success is defined only by appearance, it often leads to overextension and emotional disconnection.

A life built on borrowed definitions of success requires constant maintenance. It demands performance rather than presence. Having success requires clarity about why something matters, not merely what it looks like to others.

When success is pursued without meaning, it becomes fragile. When it is grounded in values, it becomes stable.

Defining Success Intentionally

To understand what it means to have success, reflection is essential. Many people experience success but move past it too quickly, focused on what comes next. Without recognition, success becomes invisible—even when it is real.

Pause long enough to ask yourself what success has already required of you. What did those moments feel like? What values were present when fulfillment was strongest? Success is not only something you reach; it is something you recognize and integrate.

When success is acknowledged, it stops feeling elusive and begins to feel earned.

Success, Happiness, and Emotional Awareness

Often, what people seek through success is happiness. Success becomes the vehicle, while happiness is assumed to be the destination. We associate achievement with pride, satisfaction, and joy, yet emotions are not permanent states. They shift.

This creates confusion for many who reach their goals and still feel unsettled. Success does not eliminate emotional fluctuation—it introduces responsibility for managing it. Achievement changes conditions, not emotional complexity.

Happiness cannot be captured and preserved. It must be experienced and renewed. Having success requires emotional awareness—the ability to remain grounded as circumstances change and expectations evolve.

When we ask whether we can *have* success, we are often asking whether we can live with meaning, steadiness, and self-respect once achievement arrives. The answer is yes—but only with intention.

Navigating the Complexity of Having More

As success expands, complexity often increases. Responsibilities grow, expectations shift, and relationships evolve. Financial or professional advancement can surface differences in values or priorities that once went unnoticed, requiring greater discernment and emotional range.

Having success requires maturity—the ability to separate worth from wealth, identity from status, and values from outcomes. Compatibility matters in both personal and professional relationships, and growth exposes misalignment with clarity rather than judgment. Relationships built on convenience or gain rarely survive expansion, while those rooted in authenticity, respect, and shared vision are more likely to endure over time.

Courage, Clarity, and Continuation

Having success does not eliminate fear. It often introduces new versions of it—fear of loss, visibility, responsibility, or change. Courage is required not only to pursue success, but to inhabit it fully and remain present as conditions evolve.

Many people retreat at this stage, shrinking themselves to pre-serve comfort or familiarity. This withdrawal is usually driven by assumption rather than evidence. Growth requires confronting confusion directly, addressing misunderstandings, and removing masks—both internal and external. Avoidance stalls success, while clarity sustains it.

Gratitude as a Stabilizing Force

Gratitude anchors success by restoring perspective. When effort, progress, and growth are acknowledged, emotional stability increases. Gratitude does not deny challenges; it places them in context and prevents success from becoming brittle.

Obstacles are not proof of failure. They are part of refinement, strengthening discernment, resilience, and capacity. When success is approached with gratitude rather than entitlement, it becomes sus-tainable. Celebrating progress—without inflating ego or minimizing effort—keeps success grounded and integrated.

Success as Impact and Legacy

Having success is not only about attainment; it is about influence. Impact gives success longevity. What you build matters less than how it shapes others and what continues because of your presence.

Legacy is not created through recognition alone, but through example. Success is reflected in what others learn from you, how they grow around you, and what is strengthened through your choices. True success leaves traces—in character, in courage, and in lives qui-etly supported and expanded.

Sustaining What You Have

Sustaining success requires continued vision. Reaching a goal does not signal completion; it introduces a new responsibility—to remain engaged with growth rather than settling into comfort. When

momentum pauses for too long, stagnation quietly erodes fulfillment. Evolution, not arrival, preserves vitality.

Success is not a fixed destination to be reached and defended.
It is a state of engagement, lived through awareness, gratitude, and
responsibility. Awareness keeps perspective clear. Gratitude anchors
success in humility rather than entitlement. Responsibility ensures
that what has been built is cared for rather than consumed.

To have success is to recognize it without clinging, to honor it
without complacency, and to steward it with wisdom. What is sustained intentionally does not fade with time; it matures. When success is approached as a living practice rather than a final achievement,
it remains expansive, grounded, and capable of evolving alongside
the person who carries it.

THE SHIFT

Having success is often imagined as arrival—a moment
when effort eases, uncertainty resolves, and satisfaction settles in permanently. Yet success, once attained, rarely behaves
this way. It does not pause life. It enters it. And when it does,
it introduces new responsibilities, expectations, and internal
adjustments that few people anticipate.

Success changes how you are perceived. It alters how
you are relied upon. It reshapes what is expected of you—by
others and by yourself. What once motivated you may no
longer feel sufficient. What once felt distant may now feel
demanding.

Having success is not the end of effort. It is the beginning
of stewardship.

Many people struggle at this stage not because success
is undeserved, but because they have not prepared emotionally for its presence. Success exposes unresolved boundaries,

unexamined beliefs, and internal narratives about worth. Without awareness, it can quietly replace fulfillment with pressure.

To have success well requires grounding. It requires the ability to enjoy progress without fully anchoring identity to outcomes. When success becomes the sole source of validation, it grows fragile. When it is integrated rather than idolized, it becomes stabilizing.

Having success is not about holding tightly.

It is about holding wisely.

⏱ A Moment in Motion

The goal has been met. The recognition arrives. The work is acknowledged. For a brief moment, there is relief—followed quickly by something less expected.

The question shifts.

What now?

Messages increase. Expectations rise. The space that once held anticipation is now filled with responsibility. Success is present, but it feels heavier than imagined. Not unwelcome—just unfamiliar.

In the quiet that follows, a realization forms: having success requires a different kind of strength than pursuing it ever did.

The Reflection

Before moving forward, pause here.
Not to celebrate excessively.
Not to dismiss what you've earned.
Simply to observe how success is currently experienced.

- How does success feel in your body and daily life—not in theory, but in practice?
- What new expectations have emerged since achieving what you once wanted?
- Where do you feel pride, and where do you feel pressure?
- What parts of yourself risk being overshadowed by success if left unattended?
- If success were something to integrate rather than protect, what would that require of you?

Having success does not guarantee satisfaction. It requires interpretation.

The way you relate to success determines whether it becomes a source of stability or strain. When success is grounded in values, it supports growth. When it is used primarily to validate worth, it becomes exhausting.

You are allowed to enjoy success without being consumed by it. You are allowed to adjust how it fits into your life. Success that cannot be lived with honesty eventually demands too much.

This chapter is not about diminishing achievement. It is about learning how to live alongside it.

Before you move on, carry this understanding forward: success is not proven by how tightly you hold it, but by how well you live within it.

And sustainability begins once success arrives.

Capacity to Receive Without Identity Collapse

Receiving success changes how you are perceived and how you relate to yourself. Without preparation, achievement can destabilize identity just as deeply as failure can.

This chapter develops the capacity to receive success without collapsing under its weight. When success is integrated rather than absorbed as identity, it becomes something you live with—rather than something you must defend.

CHAPTER EIGHT

SUSTAINING SUCCESS

> "*I expect to pass through this world but once. Any good therefore that I can do, or any kindness I can show to any fellow human being, let me do it now. Let me not defer or neglect it, for I shall not pass this way again.*"
> —Stephen Grellet

The Difference Between Having and Holding

Having success and sustaining it are two distinct experiences. Achievement is often visible and publicly acknowledged. Sustainability is quieter, more disciplined, and far more internal. While success may be reached through momentum, sustaining it requires intention.

Because success is personal, sustaining it must also be self-directed. There is no universal formula for maintaining fulfillment, relevance, or stability over time. Those who sustain success understand that it requires ongoing care, attention, and respect for the conditions that made it possible.

Sustained success is never accidental. It is built through structure, reflection, and continued development—long after applause fades and novelty disappears.

Success as a Living System

Success is not static. It functions as a living system that must be maintained, refined, and nourished over time. Like any system designed to endure, it requires regular assessment and adjustment.

Sustaining success means asking ongoing questions. How are you growing in this season? What requires refinement? Which habits are strengthening the vision, and which no longer serve it? These questions are not indicators of instability; they are evidence of engagement.

Success cannot be treated as a completed task. It must be stewarded. When curiosity disappears, stagnation follows. When reflection is neglected, erosion begins quietly.

The Role of a Living Plan

A sustainable plan provides structure without rigidity. It offers direction while allowing adaptation. When challenges arise—and they will—the plan becomes a point of return rather than a point of failure.

Writing a plan matters. Clarity deepens commitment. A written plan transforms intention into responsibility and creates space for strategic problem-solving. It allows you to respond rather than react as conditions change.

Vagueness weakens momentum. Vision without structure leads to drift. A clear plan, supported by flexible strategies, keeps success responsive rather than fragile. As growth introduces new variables, sustainability depends on the willingness to revise without abandoning core direction.

Consistency as a Trust Builder

Sustaining success requires a consistent value system. Over time, consistency builds trust—first within yourself, then with others. What is most respected in people, work, and institutions is not intensity or brilliance, but reliability grounded in integrity.

Consistency does not mean perfection. It refers to alignment among values, decisions, and behavior over time. When actions repeatedly reflect intention, success stabilizes rather than fluctuates. Trust compounds quietly through follow-through, not through declaration.

A personal mission—whether formally written or deeply internalized—serves as an anchor. When focus wavers or pressure increases, this internal standard provides orientation. It allows recalibration without abandonment of direction and steadiness without rigidity.

Self-Awareness and Recalibration

Life will test your priorities. Distraction, pressure, and fatigue are not interruptions to success; they are conditions within it. Sustaining success depends on self-awareness—the ability to notice drift early and respond before misalignment hardens into consequence.

Self-awareness allows recalibration without collapse. When identity is grounded, adjustment does not require crisis to justify it. Success erodes not from challenge itself, but from the absence of presence during challenge.

Partial engagement produces partial outcomes. Sustainability requires full participation—mentally, emotionally, and ethically. Presence protects progress by keeping intention active rather than assumed.

The Discipline of Ongoing Dialogue

Sustained success requires communication—both internal and external. Honest self-reflection keeps the inner world aligned with outward commitments. Regular check-ins create space to notice subtle shifts before they become visible disruptions.

Life is better understood as an ongoing conversation than a fixed narrative. Conditions change. Priorities evolve. Listening for what requires attention allows you to respond with intention rather than react out of habit or avoidance.

Preparation and imagination operate together. While no outcome can be fully controlled, readiness can be cultivated—financially, emotionally, and creatively. This readiness allows change to be met with composure instead of fear, and continuity to be preserved even as form evolves.

Creativity as a Renewable Resource

Creativity sustains momentum by keeping engagement alive. It renews energy, refreshes perspective, and prevents success from hardening into routine. When openness to learning is maintained—through lived experience, thoughtful dialogue, art, or quiet observation—progress remains fluid rather than rigid.

Creativity does not always appear as innovation or visible expression. Often, it shows up as adaptability, curiosity, or the capacity to see familiar challenges from a new angle. In this way, creativity becomes less about production and more about perception.

Growth rarely announces itself through dramatic transformation. More often, it arrives quietly through refined habits, improved judgment, or a deeper awareness of what truly matters. These shifts may feel insignificant in isolation, but over time they compound into stability. Creativity supports this process by allowing growth to remain responsive rather than forced. When imagination and awareness are preserved, success stays alive—capable of renewing itself as conditions change and understanding deepens.

Flow, Not Force

When success is sustained, it no longer feels like something to be chased or defended. It becomes something you participate in—an ongoing relationship rather than a distant pursuit. Effort shifts from frantic to intentional. Responsibility feels integrated rather than heavy.

Success flows when structure supports intention and intention honors growth. Systems, habits, and disciplines exist not to constrain, but to create space for expansion. When alignment is present, progress feels responsive and alive. When force replaces alignment, success weakens.

What is pushed too aggressively often fractures. What is allowed to develop within its proper rhythm gains durability. Sustaining success is not about holding tightly or preserving a static version of achievement. It is about remaining present, adaptable, and willing to evolve. Vision does not ask you to arrive once; it asks you to become—again and again—the version of yourself capable of carrying what you are building.

In flow, success is not exhausted by effort.

It is renewed through alignment.

THE SHIFT

Sustaining success requires a different discipline than achieving it.

Achievement is fueled by momentum, urgency, and aspiration. Sustainability is built through rhythm, boundaries, and discernment. What brings success into existence will not necessarily keep it intact. Without adjustment, the habits that once drove progress can quietly begin to erode it.

Many people assume sustaining success means maintaining the same pace indefinitely. In reality, it requires recalibration. Energy must be protected. Time must be reassessed. Priorities must be clarified. Success that is not adjusted for longevity becomes fragile.

Sustainability is not about holding tightly. It is about creating conditions that allow success to coexist with well-being. When pressure replaces purpose, sustainability weakens. When alignment is maintained, success becomes less demanding and more integrated.

Sustaining success also requires restraint. Not every opportunity deserves pursuit. Not every expectation warrants fulfillment. Growth without boundaries creates instability. Longevity depends on knowing when to advance and when to consolidate.

Sustaining success is not passive.

It is active maintenance—intentional, ongoing, and often invisible.

🕑 A Moment in Motion

The pace has been fast for some time. Results are steady. Recognition continues. From the outside, everything appears to be working.

Internally, however, there is a subtle strain. Recovery takes longer. Focus requires more effort. The margin that once existed between work and rest has narrowed.

Nothing has collapsed. Nothing urgent demands immediate change. Still, a quiet awareness emerges: if nothing shifts, something eventually will.

The realization is not alarming.

It is instructive.

The Reflection

Before moving forward, pause here.
Not to increase output.
Not to prove resilience.
Simply to assess sustainability honestly.

- What aspects of your current success feel stable, and which feel strained?
- Where have you maintained momentum at the expense of recovery?
- What boundaries support your success—and which ones need reinforcement?
- What pressures have quietly increased as success has grown?
- If you were designing success for longevity, what would need to change?

Sustaining success is less about effort and more about structure.

The systems you rely on—routines, relationships, expectations—either support endurance or gradually undermine it. When sustainability is neglected, success becomes a temporary condition rather than a lasting one.

You do not sustain success by doing everything yourself or by remaining constantly available. You sustain it by creating space for rest, reflection, and recalibration. Success that cannot be rested within cannot be sustained.

This chapter is not about slowing down unnecessarily. It is about ensuring that progress remains livable.

Before you move on, carry this understanding forward: sustaining success is not about maintaining intensity. It is about maintaining alignment.

Alignment is what allows success to endure.

Capacity to Carry

Success does not conclude at achievement. It demands continuity. What has been built must now be held, protected, and maintained with intention.

This chapter expands the capacity to carry success without depletion. Sustainability emerges when success is supported by structure rather than driven by momentum alone.

CHAPTER NINE

ACHIEVING SUCCESS

> 66
>
> *"Don't be afraid to take a big step when one is indicated. You can't cross a chasm in two small steps."*
> —David Lloyd George
>
> 99

When Success Arrives Quietly

A chieving success is often subtler than expected. Many people imagine success will announce itself—dramatic, visible, unmistakable. In reality, it frequently arrives without spectacle. You may not recognize it in the moment. One day simply feels different from the one before it, though nothing obvious appears to have changed.

There is no universal signal. No applause. No instant confirmation.

This is why many people achieve success without feeling successful. They wait for validation—approval from others, recognition from institutions, affirmation from critics. But success does not require consensus. It does not depend on praise or resistance. It exists independently of both.

The Shift That Cannot Be Reversed

Once a vision has been internalized, there is no returning to who you were before it. You move forward because the alternative no longer fits. Achieving success often feels less like winning and more like reaching a point of no return.

This is the moment when wishing ends and commitment begins.

Belief solidifies. Distractions lose influence. The opinions of others recede. You are no longer attempting to fit into a life—you are building one from the inside out.

The Cocoon of Belief

Achieving success requires protecting belief while it matures. Vision is most vulnerable in its early stages, not because it lacks strength, but because it has not yet developed insulation against noise. Without protection, comparison seeps in. Doubt gains access. Progress slows—not from incapacity, but from unnecessary exposure.

Belief must be allowed to strengthen privately before it can withstand external scrutiny.

Comparison is deceptive by nature. Each person moves along a distinct timeline, shaped by circumstance, readiness, and internal alignment. What appears effortless from the outside often reflects years of unseen preparation. Mastery does not announce itself early. It is cultivated quietly—through repetition, reflection, and discipline—by returning to the work long after novelty fades and attention moves elsewhere.

Mastery is not perfection. It is alignment.

It is the ongoing decision to return, again and again, to what is true. It reflects coherence between intention and action, not flawlessness. Belief deepens when effort is grounded in honesty rather than performance, and when progress is measured internally rather than against borrowed standards.

Success as an Evolving Identity

Your definition of success will evolve, and that evolution is not failure—it is evidence of growth. As awareness expands, priorities refine. What once felt essential may later feel limiting. Milestones exist not to finalize identity, but to mark movement. They remind you that progress is unfolding, even when momentum feels slow or invisible.

Success is not confined to major life events or public recognition. More often, it lives in quieter achievements: completing something you once avoided, recommitting after discouragement, continuing when no one is watching. These moments rarely receive applause, yet they form the backbone of lasting success. Over time, they shape identity—not through declaration, but through consistency. In this way, success becomes less about arrival and more about becoming—steady, intentional, and deeply owned.

The Discipline of Recognition

Many people minimize their accomplishments, believing success must be dramatic or publicly affirmed in order to be legitimate. Yet achievement is cumulative. It is built through consistency rather than spectacle, through the steady application of effort over time. Progress that unfolds quietly is no less real simply because it resists immediate celebration. Learning to recognize one's own growth is a discipline in itself—one that requires honesty, perspective, and patience.

Recognition often requires distance. Only with time—six months, a year, sometimes longer—does transformation become visible in full. What once existed only as an idea has taken form through sustained action. Skills have sharpened. Capacity has expanded. Direction has clarified. These changes may feel incremental while they are occurring, but their impact becomes undeniable when viewed in retrospect. That matters.

Others may not understand the value of what you have built. Their inability to see it does not diminish its worth. External recognition is shaped by perspective, proximity, and readiness. Your responsibility is not to persuade others of your progress, but to remain grounded in the truth of what has been developed. Their perception is not your reality.

Built in the Shadows

Success is often celebrated at its peak, yet it is constructed quietly—through effort, sacrifice, learning, and persistence carried out beyond public view. Every visible outcome rests upon unseen preparation. The hours invested, the adjustments made, and the lessons absorbed form the foundation upon which success stands.

Fundamentals cannot be bypassed. Every enduring achievement depends on skill, repetition, and readiness. Nothing that lasts is accidental, even when it appears effortless from the outside. What looks like ease is usually the result of mastery earned over time.

Success is not a single moment or milestone. It is a mosaic—vision, action, discipline, mindset, and courage assembled patiently over time. Each piece matters. Together, they create something cohesive, resilient, and deeply earned.

Courage and the Work of Fear

Achieving success requires courage, particularly the courage to confront fear directly. Not only the fear of failure, but the fear of potential—the quiet realization that you are capable of more than you have allowed yourself to become. This awareness can be unsettling. Growth disrupts familiarity, and familiarity often feels safer than expansion, even when it limits what is possible.

Fear rarely announces itself dramatically. More often, it speaks through hesitation, self-doubt, and delay. It assigns narratives designed to preserve comfort and reduce risk, encouraging restraint disguised as caution. These stories may sound reasonable, even protective, but fear does not possess authority over your future. It is information, not instruction.

Fear need not be eliminated for progress to occur. It needs to be understood. When fear is acknowledged rather than resisted, it loses its ability to dominate decision-making. Movement forward does not require certainty; it requires willingness. Courage is not the absence of fear, but the choice to act with awareness in its presence.

Reclaiming Authority Over Your Story

Many people struggle more with accepting positive truth than with enduring criticism. Limitations often feel familiar, while capability demands responsibility. It can feel easier to minimize potential than to inhabit it, because ownership invites accountability fully. Yet this avoidance quietly constrains growth.

Power is reclaimed through recognition—of effort invested, growth achieved, and capacity earned over time. Achieving success requires the ability to receive what you have worked for without deflection or dismissal. Denying progress does not create humility; it creates disconnection.

No one else gets to define your value. No one else determines your look of success. That authority cannot be transferred, outsourced, or deferred. It belongs to you. When you claim it with clarity and integrity, fear loses its grip, and progress becomes an act of self-trust rather than resistance.

Claiming What You Have Built

Achieving success is not about arrival. It concerns ownership— the willingness to stand fully within what you have built and to recognize it as yours. Ownership of your vision, not as an idea you once held, but as a direction you have lived. Ownership of your progress, including the uneven steps, the revisions, and the persistence that carried you forward. Ownership of who you have become through the process, not only of what you have produced.

Claiming success requires honesty and restraint. It asks that you acknowledge growth without comparison and without apology. What you have built does not need justification, explanation, or external validation to be real. When success is claimed internally, it stabilizes. It becomes something you can carry without defensiveness or doubt.

This act of recognition completes a cycle. It closes the gap between effort and acknowledgment, between becoming and being. From that grounded place, momentum renews itself. The next evolution does not emerge from striving, but from clarity—rooted in what has already been earned and ready to expand beyond it.

THE SHIFT

Achieving success is often misunderstood as a single moment.

A goal reached. A milestone crossed. A box finally checked. But achievement is rarely that clean. It unfolds gradually, through accumulation rather than arrival. By the time success is recognized, it has often been built quietly over time.

Many people expect achievement to feel definitive. Instead, it frequently feels subtle—sometimes even anticlimactic. The work continues. Life remains complex. New questions surface almost immediately. This does not diminish success. It clarifies it.

Achievement is not a reward for endurance. It is the outcome of repeatedly aligning. When actions, values, and effort converge over time, success becomes visible. When they do not, even impressive accomplishments feel unstable.

Achieving success requires perspective. Without reflection, achievement becomes fleeting—noticed briefly, then replaced by the next demand. When achievement is acknowledged intentionally, it becomes grounding. It provides evidence that effort mattered and direction was sound.

Achievement is not the end of striving. It is proof that progress occurred.

🕰 A Moment in Motion

The result appears quietly. No announcement. No ceremony. Just confirmation that something once imagined has now taken shape.

There is satisfaction—but it is measured. Calm rather than celebratory. The achievement feels real, yet incomplete. Almost immediately, awareness shifts forward. What was once the destination is now part of the landscape.

For a moment, there is stillness. A recognition that something meaningful has been accomplished. Then life resumes—not dismissing the achievement, but carrying it forward.

The success does not vanish. It integrates.

The Reflection

Before moving forward, pause here.
Not to rush toward the next goal.
Not to downplay what you've achieved.
Simply to recognize achievement honestly.

- What have you achieved that you rarely acknowledge?
- How do you typically respond to success—by pausing, or by immediately moving on?
- What effort or discipline made this achievement possible?

- Where does achievement feel stabilizing, and where does it feel incomplete?
- If achievement were viewed as confirmation rather than conclusion, what would you appreciate differently?

Achievement deserves recognition—not for validation, but for orientation.

When achievement is acknowledged, it reinforces trust in your capacity to follow through. When it is ignored, progress loses meaning and motivation weakens. Reflection turns achievement into learning rather than pressure.

You do not need to linger indefinitely at each milestone. But you do need to register that it occurred. Success that is never acknowledged becomes difficult to sustain.

This chapter is not about celebrating endlessly. It is about recognizing that achievement is part of a continuum—not an endpoint, but evidence of alignment in motion.

Before you move on, carry this understanding forward: achieving success is not about reaching a final state. It is about confirming that your direction has been sound.

And confirmation strengthens what comes next.

Capacity to Integrate Achievement

Achievement is often mistaken for completion. In reality, it is a moment of convergence—one that must be absorbed thoughtfully into a larger life.

This chapter strengthens the capacity to integrate achievement without allowing it to overshadow meaning, relationship, or well-being. Success that integrates rather than dominates remains grounded.

CHAPTER TEN

VARIOUS TRIALS

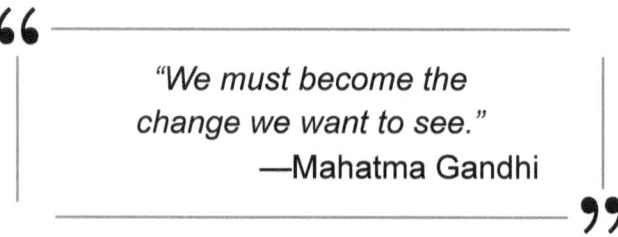

> "We must become the
> change we want to see."
> —Mahatma Gandhi

The Inevitability of Challenge

At some point, nearly everyone asks the same questions: *Why did this happen? Why now? Why this way? Why me?* These questions do not arise because life has gone wrong, but because uncertainty is an unavoidable part of being human. Life is not something we fully control or completely understand. We experience it, interpret it, and respond to it in real time—often without clarity about what comes next. Meaning is rarely immediate. More often, it sharpens only through reflection and time.

Trials are not anomalies or interruptions to an otherwise predictable life. They are woven into the human experience itself. Difficulty, loss, disruption, and resistance appear across every life path, regardless of status, preparation, or intention. The presence of challenge does not indicate failure. It signals engagement with life at a depth where growth becomes possible.

Cause, Response, and Responsibility

What individuals bring into the world—their attitudes, behaviors, expectations, and emotional energy—shapes how they experience what meets them. Internal states influence external outcomes, not always directly or immediately, but consistently over time. Through repetition, patterns emerge, revealing where alignment exists and where it has eroded. These patterns are not punishments. They are feedback.

When people commit to growth, clarity, or success, resistance often follows. This resistance does not mean the direction is wrong. It reflects the friction that naturally accompanies expansion. Pressure reveals structure. Stress exposes weak points. These moments provide information about what is stable, what is fragile, and what requires reinforcement. When interpreted accurately, they become opportunities for recalibration rather than reasons for retreat.

Trials as Developmental Pressure

Every serious pursuit invites challenge. As progress accelerates, comfort tends to decrease. Certainty dissolves. Familiar routines lose effectiveness. Resources—time, energy, or support—may shift unexpectedly. What once felt reliable may no longer be sufficient. These moments feel destabilizing not because something is broken, but because growth has outpaced existing structures.

Trials force reassessment. They ask essential questions: *What still works? What no longer fits? What must be strengthened? What must be released?* Growth requires adjustment. Without it, advancement stalls and momentum becomes unsustainable. Developmental pressure is not designed to break what is strong. It reveals what must evolve in order to continue.

Meaning Is Made, Not Given

Trials do not arrive with explanations attached. Meaning is not delivered alongside difficulty; it is constructed through response.

Some people collapse inward when disruption appears. Others reorient, adapt, and rebuild. The difference lies not in circumstance, but in interpretation and action. What an individual believes about a trial shapes how they move through it.

Suffering is universal rather than selective. No one is uniquely targeted, and no one is exempt. What varies is how difficulty is processed and what is built from it. Over time, the same experience can either diminish capacity or deepen it, depending on how responsibility, reflection, and choice are applied.

THE SHIFT

Trials do not arrive as invitations. They arrive as interruptions. They disrupt rhythm, challenge identity, and force reassessment—often at moments when progress appears secure. Trials are not evidence that something has gone wrong. They are evidence that something real is being tested. For those whose lives carry responsibility, visibility, or influence, trials often arrive quietly but carry significant weight. There is rarely space to pause publicly, even when recalibration is required privately.

Not all trials announce themselves through crisis or collapse. Some surface subtly: a gradual loss of motivation, a quiet shift in values, or an increasing sense that what once fit no longer does. These moments are easily dismissed, yet they are often the most instructive. They signal the need for adjustment before erosion becomes visible. Trials do not negate success. They refine it—clarifying what must be strengthened, released, or reoriented in order for growth to continue with integrity.

⏰ A Moment in Motion

At a point when life appeared stable from the outside, a seasoned professional became aware that something subtle but persistent had shifted internally. The accomplishments remained intact, the role carried respect, and financial footing was secure. Yet the sense of alignment that once made effort feel purposeful had quietly eroded. There was no public failure, no dramatic loss, and no explanation that could be offered without sounding ungrateful.

Decisions that once felt intuitive now required strain. Momentum that once energized now depleted. The issue was not competence or capability; it was capacity. What had been built still stood, but sustaining it now demanded a different internal structure than the one that had supported earlier success. The trial was not about endurance or pushing harder. It was about recalibration.

Recognizing that distinction did not invalidate what had already been achieved. It clarified what needed to evolve next. In this moment, growth did not require persistence alone, but discernment—the willingness to adjust internally in order to continue forward with integrity.

The Reflection

Before moving forward, pause here.
Not to explain the trial.
Not to assign meaning too quickly.
Simply to acknowledge what is present.

- What pressures are you currently navigating that few people see?
- How has success complicated this season rather than simplified it?
- What part of your identity feels most tested right now?
- Where are you holding together externally while fragmenting internally?
- If this trial is asking for recalibration rather than endurance, what might need to change?

Trials demand honesty before strategy.

When trials are ignored, they intensify. When they are acknowledged, they become instructive. Growth often begins not with resolution, but with permission to adjust.

Capacity to Recalibrate

Trials interrupt trajectory, but they do not invalidate progress. They test assumptions and reveal where adjustment is required. This chapter builds the capacity to recalibrate rather than retreat. When trials are engaged with discernment, success evolves rather than erodes.

CHAPTER ELEVEN

MONEY

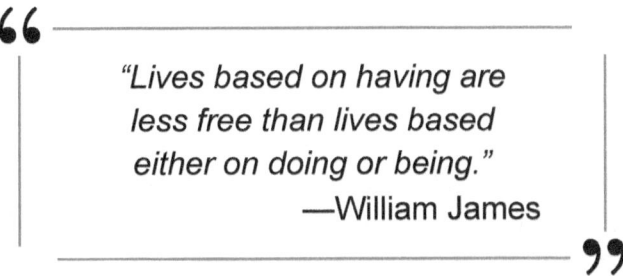

"Lives based on having are less free than lives based either on doing or being."
—William James

Money as Context, Not Identity

Money tends to appear in life in two primary forms: having enough to support forward movement, or not having enough to do so comfortably. Most people live somewhere between these states, navigating trade-offs that shape time, energy, and choice. While financial circumstances differ widely, the emotional relationship people have with money is often strikingly similar.

Money is rarely neutral. It carries pressure, comparison, fear, expectation, and deeply held assumptions about worth and capability. Yet money itself is not the problem. The problem lies in what people believe money represents—and what they allow it to define.

When money becomes identity rather than context, clarity erodes. Decisions begin to serve appearance rather than purpose.

Freedom narrows, even as resources increase. Wealth without discernment does not expand choice; it complicates it.

When Money Is Available

Having sufficient money to support your goals creates flexibility. It removes certain constraints and allows attention to shift from survival to execution. This can be a powerful position—if it is handled with intention rather than impulse.

Access to money does not automatically create freedom. When lifestyle expands faster than clarity, "enough" becomes a moving target. Consumption quietly replaces purpose. The effort once directed toward growth becomes absorbed by maintenance. Money earned solely to meet expectations or preserve image often produces anxiety rather than security.

When money begins to dictate identity, it assumes control over decision-making. Choices narrow around preservation rather than possibility. In this state, abundance can quietly become restrictive— binding effort to upkeep instead of progress.

When Money Is Limited

For many, the challenge is not excess, but restriction. Limited funds compress options and narrow focus. When income barely sustains existing obligations, creativity feels risky. Vision is postponed. Growth is labeled impractical.

This is where many people quietly abandon their goals—not because desire disappears, but because the conditions feel unsustainable. Financial pressure convinces people to delay life rather than redesign it. Survival becomes the priority, and expansion is framed as irresponsible rather than necessary.

Yet lack of money does not equal lack of agency. Constraint changes strategy, not capacity. When approached with discernment rather than defeat, limitation can clarify priorities and sharpen intention rather than extinguish them.

The Real Constraint: Time and Energy

Financial limitation is often intensified not by lack of ability, but by scarcity of time and energy. When most hours are consumed maintaining stability—meeting obligations, managing responsibilities, sustaining daily function—little capacity remains for creation or long-term vision. The constraint is not always income itself, but the exhaustion that accompanies survival-mode living.

Taking on more work may increase income temporarily, but it often reduces the very capacity required to build something lasting. Additional hours can generate short-term relief while quietly eroding the energy needed for strategic thinking, creativity, and sustained follow-through. Over time, this imbalance creates a familiar cycle: not enough money to invest, not enough time to create, and not enough energy to persist.

Breaking this cycle rarely requires dramatic upheaval. It requires strategic adjustment—small, deliberate shifts that reclaim margin. Space to think. Space to plan. Space to act with intention rather than urgency. Even modest changes in how time and energy are allocated can restore momentum by creating breathing room where none previously existed.

Money as a Tool, Not a Measure

Money is a tool. It amplifies what already exists—clarity or confusion, intention or avoidance. Used consciously, it supports choice, stability, and expansion. Used unconsciously, it magnifies anxiety and distraction.

When money is treated as proof of worth, it becomes emotionally loaded and difficult to hold. When it is treated as a resource to be managed in service of values, it becomes stabilizing. Financial health is less about accumulation than alignment—between income, intention, and lifestyle.

The question is not how much money you have. It is how money moves through your life, and what it is being asked to support.

Stewardship Over Scarcity

Whether money is abundant or constrained, stewardship matters. Stewardship replaces fear with responsibility. It asks not *how much* you have, but *how intentionally* you use it.

Sustainable success requires financial awareness without fixation. It requires planning without rigidity, ambition without compulsion, and restraint without deprivation. Money serves best when it is positioned as support rather than signal—context rather than identity.

This chapter is not about wealth or poverty. It is about orientation. When money is placed in proper relationship to purpose, it stops distorting decision-making and starts enabling it.

Money does not define who you are. It reveals how you choose.

Passion Is Not a Substitute—But It Is a Catalyst

Passion is not a replacement for income, nor does it eliminate practical realities. However, it plays a critical role when resources are limited. Passion sustains momentum when external reinforcement is minimal. It sharpens focus, encourages creative problem-solving, and opens pathways to collaboration and unconventional solutions that would otherwise remain unseen.

Many meaningful ventures begin without capital. They do not start with ideal conditions, abundant funding, or guaranteed outcomes. They begin with commitment, consistency, and the willingness to proceed despite uncertainty. Money can accelerate progress once movement is underway, but it rarely initiates it. Initiation comes from belief paired with action.

What matters most is not perfection or readiness, but the decision to continue. Progress compounds when effort is sustained, even imperfectly. When time and energy are protected with intention, and passion is allowed to catalyze movement rather than replace structure, growth becomes possible—even within constraint.

Resourcefulness Over Resignation

Money is one resource—not the only one. Skills, networks, adaptability, reduced expenses, shared opportunities, and incremental progress all matter. Often, the obstacle is not a lack of money, but rigid assumptions about how success must unfold.

Progress does not require certainty. It requires movement.

Waiting for financial security before acting often delays growth indefinitely. Moving thoughtfully within constraint builds confidence, capability, and resilience.

Money as a Tool, Not a Verdict

Money can motivate short-term behavior, but it cannot sustain purpose. Financial disruptions are inevitable, regardless of preparation. Unexpected costs arise, obligations shift, and circumstances change in ways that disrupt even the most careful plans. If money alone determines whether progress continues, then progress will always remain fragile. Purpose that depends entirely on financial stability collapses the moment instability appears.

Money does not define readiness, worth, or the legitimacy of a vision. Resources can support execution, but they do not confer meaning or direction. Even with unlimited funding, nothing moves without action. Ideas remain inert without awareness, effort, and clarity. It is not money that brings vision into form, but the willingness to engage consistently with the work required to build it.

The Myth That Money Is the Barrier

Money is frequently blamed for stalled dreams, yet more often it serves as a justification for delay rather than a true obstacle. Financial limitations may slow progress, but they rarely halt it entirely. Many initiatives begin under constrained conditions and advance incrementally, guided more by commitment than by capital. When progress stops completely, the cause is usually internal rather than financial.

What consistently blocks momentum is hesitation, fear, and the belief that permission is required before movement can begin. Waiting for ideal conditions often disguises avoidance as prudence. While money matters, it is not the gatekeeper of possibility. Progress responds first to decision, then to effort, and only later to resources. When action leads, support has a way of finding its place.

Moving Forward With Clarity

A healthy relationship with money is rooted in clarity. This clarity comes from knowing the difference between what is necessary and what is merely desirable, understanding one's current stage of development, and making decisions that align with values rather than pressure or fear. When financial choices are grounded in self-awareness, they support stability instead of anxiety and direction instead of reaction.

When money is treated as a tool, it becomes manageable. It can be planned for, adjusted, and integrated into a broader strategy without overwhelming decision-making. When money is treated as a verdict on potential or worth, however, it becomes paralyzing. Fear replaces judgment, and hesitation begins to masquerade as caution. Progress slows not because options are unavailable, but because clarity has been compromised.

Progress is built by continuing—strategically, intentionally, and often imperfectly. Movement does not require ideal conditions; it requires direction and follow-through. Money may influence the pace at which progress unfolds, but it should never determine its direction. When clarity leads and values anchor decisions, forward motion remains possible regardless of circumstance.

THE SHIFT

Money is rarely just about money.

It carries meaning far beyond numbers—security, freedom, status, control, fear, possibility. It reflects not only what you earn or spend, but what you believe about worth, safety, and success. Because of this, money has the power to clarify priorities—or quietly distort them when left unexamined.

For some, money represents relief from instability. For others, it represents responsibility, expectation, or visibility. For many, it holds all of these meanings at once. The role money plays in your life is shaped less by how much you have and more by how consciously you relate to it. Two people with identical resources can experience entirely different levels of freedom, pressure, or satisfaction.

Money can expand options, but it does not resolve internal conflict. It may remove certain constraints while introducing new ones—greater responsibility, heightened scrutiny, or increased fear of loss. Without clarity, financial success amplifies pressure rather than peace. With clarity, money becomes a tool—useful, flexible, and subordinate to intention rather than dominant over it.

The challenge, then, is not accumulation alone. It is alignment.

When money is treated as proof of success, it becomes fragile—something that must be defended, displayed, or justified. When it is treated as a resource that supports values, purpose, and choice, it becomes stabilizing. Money is neither virtue nor failure. It is leverage. And leverage, when handled without discernment, magnifies imbalance as easily as it magnifies opportunity.

🕐 A Moment in Motion

The numbers are solid. Accounts are stable. From the outside, everything appears secure.

Yet decisions feel heavier than expected. Each choice carries weight—impacting not just lifestyle, but relationships, responsibilities, and future direction. Money no longer represents possibility alone. It represents a consequence.

There is no panic. No scarcity. Just the quiet awareness that financial success requires intention to remain supportive rather than controlling.

The realization settles: money is present, but meaning must still be chosen.

The Reflection

Before moving forward, pause here.
Not to budget.
Not to plan.
Simply to examine your relationship with money honestly.

- What does money represent to you beyond its practical function?
- Where does money provide freedom, and where does it create pressure?
- What beliefs about success and worth are reinforced by your financial reality?

- How has money changed your decision-making—for better or for strain?
- If money were treated as a support for your life rather than a measure of it, what would shift?

Money reflects priorities, whether you intend it to or not.

The way you earn, spend, save, and give reinforces what you value. When money is managed without awareness, it quietly dictates choices. When it is managed intentionally, it supports autonomy rather than controlling it.

Financial success does not require detachment from ambition. It requires integration. You are allowed to want wealth without letting it define you. You are allowed to pursue financial growth without sacrificing coherence.

This chapter is not about rejecting money or idealizing it. It is about restoring agency in how it functions within your life.

Before you move on, carry this understanding forward: money is a powerful tool, but it is not a substitute for clarity.

And success is measured by how well your resources serve your life—not the other way around.

Capacity to Relate Without Dependence

Money amplifies what already exists—values, habits, fears, and priorities. When money becomes a mirror for worth, it destabilizes identity. When it is treated as a tool, it clarifies choice.

This chapter strengthens the capacity to relate to money without dependence. Financial success becomes sustainable when it supports life rather than defines it.

CHAPTER TWELVE

MOTIVATION

> 66
>
> *"My greatest mistake, the fault for which I can't forgive myself, is that one day I ceased my obstinate pursuit of my own individuality."*
> —Oscar Wilde
>
> 99

The Question Beneath Motivation

What truly drives you?

What moves you to act when effort is required and outcomes remain uncertain?

If that question does not immediately yield an answer, motivation may still exist—but without definition. Motivation is not urgency, noise, or pressure. It is clarity sustained by commitment. It is the internal decision to continue even when reinforcement is absent and results are delayed.

Motivation begins with desire, but it endures through meaning. Without meaning, effort fragments. With meaning, effort stabilizes and direction holds even when momentum slows.

Hunger as Direction, Not Desperation

Motivation is often confused with intensity. Intensity is visible and dramatic, but it fades quickly. What endures is hunger—a quiet, personal reason to persist that does not depend on urgency or external reward.

Hunger is not desperation. It is alignment. It is the internal recognition that something matters enough to continue through uncertainty, disruption, and delay. When motivation is tied solely to recognition, approval, or reward, it weakens under pressure. When it is tied to purpose, it becomes resilient.

Purpose organizes effort. It gives direction to endurance. It allows persistence to remain steady rather than exhausting, intentional rather than reactive.

The Power of Belief

Motivation is strengthened by belief, particularly belief reflected back by others. Sometimes a single voice—offered at the right moment—is enough to confirm what is already sensed internally. That confirmation can sustain momentum when doubt threatens focus.

However, belief borrowed from others is never permanent. Over time, motivation must become self-sustaining. It must move from being reinforced externally to being anchored internally. The strongest motivation does not rely on applause or consensus. It relies on conviction that remains intact regardless of visibility.

When belief is owned rather than borrowed, effort becomes less fragile. Progress continues even when validation disappears.

Motivation Through Resistance

Motivation is often forged through resistance rather than comfort. When obstacles appear, motivation is tested—not because progress has ended, but because commitment is being examined. Discouragement, skepticism, and exclusion frequently surface when direction begins to solidify.

These experiences are not signals to stop. They are invitations to clarify resolve. Resistance exposes intention. It reveals whether a vision is cosmetic—held loosely and easily abandoned—or foundational to one's sense of purpose.

When challenges persist, motivation either erodes or deepens. It deepens when the decision is made that direction is not negotiable, even when conditions become unfavorable and outcomes remain uncertain.

Motivation Is Not Comfort-Based

True motivation does not emerge from ease or convenience. It emerges from responsibility—responsibility for one's future, one's choices, and one's growth. Comfort may spark interest, but responsibility sustains effort.

Motivation asks difficult questions that cannot be answered abstractly. What are you willing to sacrifice? What forms of discomfort can you endure without abandoning direction? What matters enough to justify persistence when progress feels slow or invisible?

Each person must answer these questions individually. Motivation strengthens when ownership replaces expectation and when responsibility is accepted without resentment.

Solitude and Self-Trust

At some point, motivation becomes solitary. Support thins. Encouragement grows quieter. External validation may disappear entirely. This shift is not punishment or abandonment; it is preparation.

Growth eventually requires standing without reinforcement. Learning to continue without affirmation develops self-trust. Motivation matures when it no longer depends on reassurance or approval. It becomes quieter, steadier, and less reactive to praise or doubt.

Action is no longer driven by visibility or recognition. It is driven by alignment with who you are becoming. You act not because someone is watching, but because the work is consistent with your internal direction.

Motivation as Identity

Motivation is not something that must be summoned repeatedly through emotion or force. Over time, it becomes integrated. When vision merges with identity, effort feels purposeful rather than imposed.

At this stage, internal dialogue shifts. You stop questioning whether you should continue. You continue because stopping would contradict your sense of self. Motivation becomes orientation rather than intensity—less about feeling driven and more about remaining coherent.

When motivation reaches this stage, effort no longer requires persuasion. It becomes expression.

The Risk of Commitment

Motivation requires risk. To commit fully to a vision is to accept uncertainty and the possibility of misalignment or failure. There is no guarantee of outcome and no promise of ease.

Avoidance preserves comfort but guarantees stagnation. Progress belongs to those willing to try, adjust, and continue. Motivation does not eliminate fear—it outpaces it.

The decisive moment remains the same across every pursuit: move forward or retreat. That choice, repeated consistently, shapes everything that follows.

Sustaining the Fire

Motivation is sustained through clear purpose, honest self-reflection, and alignment between values and action. It also requires a willingness to endure discomfort without abandoning direction. Fatigue will surface. Doubt will appear. These experiences are not signs of failure; they are part of sustained effort.

Belief, even in small amounts, has a compounding effect. It builds momentum quietly, carrying progress forward when certainty is unavailable. Over time, belief becomes sturdier than confidence, because it persists without needing proof.

Living the Decision

Motivation is not defined by dramatic sacrifice or reckless risk. It is expressed through daily alignment—showing up, continuing, choosing again. The work is often ordinary, repetitive, and unseen. What makes it meaningful is consistency.

Dreams do not require perfection. They require participation. When something matters deeply enough, strength emerges gradually through action itself. Even when conditions are imperfect and outcomes remain unclear, commitment creates movement. That sustained willingness to continue is what motivation truly is.

THE SHIFT

Motivation is often treated as a constant to be maintained. People search for it, wait for it, or blame its absence when progress slows. This misunderstanding creates unnecessary frustration and self-judgment, as though motivation were a personal flaw rather than a responsive state. Motivation is not a stable resource; it fluctuates in response to meaning, fatigue, clarity, and context.

Motivation responds to purpose more than pressure. When effort is connected to values, motivation stabilizes even when energy dips or progress slows. When effort is driven by obligation, fear, or comparison, motivation erodes—regardless of discipline, talent, or ambition. Pressure may produce short bursts of action, but it cannot sustain direction without cost.

Sustainable motivation is not fueled by intensity. It is supported by relevance. When goals remain meaningful, motivation returns after pauses and disruption. When goals lose relevance, motivation fades—not as failure, but as information. This loss of drive is not a character defect; it is feedback indicating that effort is no longer aligned with purpose.

Motivation does not disappear without reason. It signals misalignment, exhaustion, unresolved conflict, or the need for recalibration. Ignoring that signal leads to self-betrayal—forcing movement when clarity is absent. Listening to it allows progress to continue with integrity rather than resentment.

Motivation is not something to force into existence. It is something to understand, interpret, and respond to wisely. When motivation is treated as guidance rather than pressure, it becomes a reliable ally rather than a recurring obstacle.

🕑 A Moment in Motion

The routine is familiar. The tasks are known. The structure is intact. Yet engagement feels thinner than before.

There is no lack of ability. No lack of opportunity. Just a quiet resistance where enthusiasm once lived. Pushing harder produces compliance, not momentum.

In a rare pause, the realization emerges: the issue is not discipline, but meaning. The work still matters—but the reason for doing it needs to be revisited.

Nothing stops. But something begins to shift.

The Reflection

Before moving forward, pause here.
Not to generate enthusiasm.
Not to criticize yourself.
Simply to observe how motivation currently operates.

- What activities or goals reliably renew your motivation?
- Where has motivation declined, and what might that be signaling?
- How often do you rely on pressure or urgency to stay engaged?
- What would change if motivation were treated as information rather than a requirement?
- If your motivation had to be sustainable rather than constant, what would you adjust?

Motivation does not need to be permanent to be effective.

When motivation is respected, it becomes a guide rather than a demand. It helps you distinguish between persistence and overextension. When it is ignored, progress continues briefly before stalling.

You are not required to feel motivated at every stage. You are required to remain honest about what fuels you and what drains you. Discipline sustains effort; motivation determines whether that effort feels worthwhile.

This chapter is not about chasing inspiration. It is about restoring coherence between intention and action.

Before you move on, carry this understanding forward: motivation is not proof of commitment. It is feedback about alignment.

And success is sustained when feedback is taken seriously.

Capacity to Reignite

Motivation is not constant. It rises, fades, and reshapes itself across seasons. When motivation is expected to remain fixed, disappointment follows.

This chapter builds the capacity to reignite motivation without self-judgment. Sustainable progress relies not on intensity, but on the ability to reconnect purpose when momentum slows.

CHAPTER THIRTEEN

SKILLS

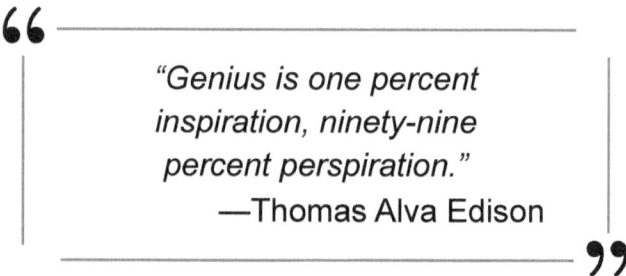

> *"Genius is one percent inspiration, ninety-nine percent perspiration."*
> —Thomas Alva Edison

Skill as the Engine of Sustainability

Talent may open doors, but skill is what keeps them open. Success that endures is never carried by potential alone. It is sustained by competence—developed, refined, and renewed over time. Skill allows success to mature rather than fracture under pressure. Without it, even the most promising trajectory eventually collapses beneath its own weight.

Skill is not static. It requires attentiveness to change, humility in learning, and willingness to evolve. The world does not pause for past achievement. Industries shift. Expectations rise. Contexts transform. Those who sustain success understand that skill must expand alongside relevance. Mastery is not a destination reached once, but a discipline practiced continuously.

Staying informed is part of skill. So is understanding the lineage of your craft—what shaped it, what failed, what endured, and why. Innovation rarely appears in isolation. It emerges from knowledge applied with discernment. Skill bridges vision and execution, turning intention into reliability. It is what allows success to move beyond momentum and become durable.

Natural Ability and Learned Competence

Everyone possesses ability, but it does not emerge uniformly. Some skills arrive naturally—instinctive, intuitive, seemingly effortless. Others are built deliberately through repetition, study, and disciplined effort. Both matter. Neither is sufficient on its own.

Natural ability is often undervalued because it feels easy to the person who holds it. Learned competence is sometimes overvalued because it requires visible sacrifice. True mastery integrates both. Effort without intuition becomes rigid. Talent without discipline becomes complacent. Sustainability lives in the balance between what comes naturally and what is consciously strengthened.

Skill matures when ability and effort are no longer in competition. When intuition is refined through structure, and discipline is guided by insight, performance stabilizes. Growth becomes reliable rather than sporadic. Confidence deepens without hardening.

Skill and Identity

Over time, skill reshapes identity. How you think, speak, analyze, create, and respond becomes woven into who you are. When skill aligns with character, presence feels grounded and authentic. Performance carries integrity rather than tension. When skill and identity are misaligned, dissonance emerges—often subtle at first, but increasingly costly.

Skill without humility distorts perspective. Mastery without self-awareness inflates ego. Overidentification with ability creates fragility, making feedback feel threatening and adaptation feel unnecessary. The relationship you have with your skill determines not only how you perform, but how you listen, lead, and evolve.

Sustainable success requires competence paired with restraint. Skill must serve purpose rather than replace it. When capability is guided by integrity, influence stabilizes and trust compounds.

Power, Passion, and Restraint

Skill carries power. Power requires management. Passion fuels growth, but unchecked passion often eclipses judgment. The goal is not intensity. It is coherence.

Those who sustain success learn to channel passion without allowing it to consume identity. They remain curious without becoming reactive. Confident without becoming rigid. Skilled without becoming untouchable. They understand that restraint is not limitation—it is control.

When passion and restraint are balanced, effort becomes sustainable. Growth remains intentional rather than compulsive. Skill no longer demands constant proof. It speaks through consistency, composure, and the quiet authority of someone who knows their craft—and continues to refine it.

Late-Blooming Skills and Rediscovery

Some skills surface later in life, not because they were absent, but because they were dormant, discouraged, or overshadowed by responsibility. Early demands often prioritize survival, compliance, or practicality, leaving little room for exploration. As awareness deepens and life experience accumulates, space opens for rediscovery. Creative expression, leadership capacity, craftsmanship, or intellectual pursuits once set aside begin to reemerge, not as hobbies, but as meaningful extensions of identity.

Skill development is not limited by age or circumstance. Growth does not expire. What matters is the willingness to begin and the commitment to continue once momentum is established. Many people discover their most impactful skills only after experience clarifies what truly matters. Perspective refines focus, and focus directs effort toward abilities that align with purpose rather than performance.

Faith, Practice, and Progression

Belief is foundational, but belief alone is insufficient. Skill is what translates faith into form. To build a livelihood—or a life—around your abilities, trust in the process must be paired with consistent practice and measurable improvement. Confidence grows not from assumption, but from repetition, refinement, and earned competence.

Learning does not end at any fixed milestone. When development stops, stagnation follows. When creation pauses, momentum fades. Progress belongs to those who remain active—mentally, creatively, and strategically—continually sharpening what they know while remaining open to what they have yet to master. There is no final arrival point. There is only refinement, carried forward through sustained engagement and deliberate growth.

Fulfillment Beyond Achievement

Many reach milestones only to discover dissatisfaction. Titles, income, and recognition do not guarantee fulfillment. Skill development keeps purpose alive. It sustains engagement rather than emptiness.

Fulfillment comes from alignment—between what you do, how you do it, and why it matters. Skill sharpens that alignment. It creates meaning beyond accomplishment and depth beyond appearance.

Protecting Growth

Not everyone will understand your evolution. Some will question it, and others may quietly resist it. Growth disrupts familiar dynamics and challenges assumptions that people have grown comfortable holding about you. This resistance is not always malicious, but it can be destabilizing if left unexamined. Recognizing this reality is part of maturing into your next stage with clarity rather than defensiveness.

Skill development requires protection. Growth does not flourish in environments that undermine learning, trivialize effort, or distort focus. Choosing contexts that reinforce discipline and curiosity matters. Feedback should strengthen discernment, not distract from direction. Progress should be acknowledged without becoming complacent, and encouragement should never replace self-trust. External validation can support growth, but it cannot sustain it. Growth thrives where intention is protected and agency is preserved.

Commitment to the Craft

Skill demands effort that is both practical and sustained. Progress requires using the resources available, making thoughtful compromises when necessary, and adapting intelligently to constraints. However, there are nonnegotiables. Learning, quality, and growth cannot be compromised without eroding the foundation of what is being built.

Mastery is not sudden or dramatic. It is built through consistency, discipline, and patience applied over time. The investment compounds quietly. What feels incremental in the present becomes foundational in hindsight. Each repetition strengthens capacity, and each refinement deepens confidence earned through practice rather than assertion.

The Foundation of the Look of Success

The look of success is not sustained by appearance alone. It rests on competence, adaptability, faith, and disciplined action. Skills give substance to vision. They make progress repeatable rather than accidental and allow success to be rebuilt when circumstances change.

What you build through skill cannot be taken from you. It becomes portable, resilient, and enduring. Carry it forward deliberately—one refinement, one lesson, one considered action at a time. This is how success becomes not only visible, but sustainable.

THE SHIFT

Skills are the quiet infrastructure of success.

They translate intention into capability and aspiration into execution. Without skill, effort depends on willpower alone—fragile, inconsistent, and easily exhausted. With skill, progress becomes repeatable. Sustainable success is rarely distinguished by raw talent; it is defined by the disciplined cultivation of the skills required to support the life being built.

Many people underestimate skills because they are largely invisible. Outcomes are celebrated. Processes are not. Results are recognized; skill-building happens quietly, often without acknowledgment. Yet every advancement, adaptation, and reinvention rests on capabilities that were once undeveloped and intentionally strengthened over time.

Skills are not static assets to be acquired and stored. They require maintenance, relevance, and renewal. What worked in one season may become insufficient in another. As environments shift, expectations evolve, and responsibility increases, skill must evolve alongside them. The ability to learn, unlearn, and relearn is not supplemental—it is essential, especially during periods of transition or expansion.

Developing skill is not an admission of inadequacy. It is an acknowledgment of growth. Those who sustain success understand that refinement is not a correction of weakness, but a response to evolution. Skill signals respect—for the work, for the process, and for the future being shaped through it.

🕰 A Moment in Motion

The environment has changed. Expectations have shifted. Familiar strategies no longer produce the same results.

There is no failure—just friction. A sense that current capabilities no longer fully match the demands of the moment. The instinct is to work harder, but something else is required: adaptation.

Attention turns to learning again. Awkward at first. Slower than expected. But with each adjustment, confidence begins to return—not from mastery, but from momentum.

The skill gap narrows. Progress resumes.

The Reflection

Before moving forward, pause here.
Not to judge your competence.
Not to compare yourself to others.
Simply to assess your current skill landscape honestly.

- What skills most directly support the success you are pursuing now?
- Which skills have become outdated or less relevant?
- Where are you relying on experience rather than continued learning?
- What skills feel uncomfortable to develop—and why?

- If growth required one new skill this season, what would it be?

Skills compound quietly.

When skill development is intentional, confidence grows without force. When it is neglected, effort increases while effectiveness declines. Skill gaps do not announce themselves loudly; they appear as resistance, inefficiency, or frustration.

You are not required to master everything. You are required to remain teachable. The ability to adapt your skills as circumstances change determines how well success evolves with you.

This chapter is not about proving capability. It is about maintaining relevance.

Before you move on, carry this understanding forward: skills are not a measure of worth. They are tools for expression.

And success depends on how well your tools match your vision.

Capacity to Compound

Skills grow quietly. Their value multiplies over time, often unnoticed until they are needed most. Mastery is rarely dramatic—it is cumulative.

This chapter develops the capacity to compound skill rather than chase immediacy. Success deepens when competence is built steadily instead of rushed publicly.

CHAPTER FOURTEEN

LEARN TO ASK

> "Most people never run far
> enough on their first wind to
> find out they've got a second.
> Give your dreams all you've
> got and you'll be amazed at the
> energy that comes out of you."
> —William James

The Courage of Inquiry

Asking is one of the most underused skills in personal and professional growth—not because people do not need answers, but because asking requires clarity, humility, and courage. Many hesitate out of fear: fear of rejection, fear of appearing uninformed, fear of hearing an answer they are not yet ready to face. And so they stall—guessing, assuming, and waiting—when a single, well-placed question could create immediate movement.

Avoidance often masquerades as patience. Silence is mistaken for strategy. But progress rarely rewards hesitation disguised as restraint.

If you intend not only to build success but to sustain it, learning how to ask is not optional. It is essential.

Asking as a Skill, Not a Personality Trait

Some people appear naturally confident in asking for clarity, access, or support. Others experience discomfort even when confusion is costly. But asking is not a personality trait—it is a skill. And skills can be developed through intention and practice.

Asking keeps momentum alive. It interrupts stagnation before it hardens. It sharpens thinking by forcing articulation rather than assumption. Most people do not fall behind because they lack intelligence or potential; they fall behind because they spend too long trying to figure out what could have been clarified in minutes. Confusion compounds quietly. Questions interrupt it.

Better Questions Create Better Outcomes

The quality of your outcomes is directly influenced by the quality of your questions. Effective questions are not vague requests for reassurance; they are directional prompts that generate movement. You do not ask simply to be comforted. You ask to become clearer.

When progress feels blocked, the first adjustment is rarely effort—it is inquiry. Refine the question. Ask again. Precision matters. Better questions produce better decisions. Better decisions restore confidence—not because certainty is guaranteed, but because direction is regained.

Reframing the Question Restores Power

Often, the obstacle is not a lack of answers, but a poorly framed question. When life is framed through powerlessness, the questions that follow reinforce it. When life is framed through responsibility, inquiry opens options.

Shift from asking why life is happening to you and begin asking what life is requiring from you. Shift from asking why you are stuck and begin asking what information, skill, or boundary is missing. This reframing restores agency. It converts frustration into forward motion.

Asking Others—and Asking Yourself

Some questions require collaboration. Trusted perspectives reveal blind spots that cannot be accessed alone. Thoughtful dialogue accelerates clarity in ways isolation cannot.

But the most consequential questions are often internal. What are you avoiding? What truth are you postponing? What needs to be released in order for movement to resume? These questions demand honesty rather than advice. When practiced consistently, that honesty becomes grounding rather than destabilizing. It strengthens self-trust and sharpens discernment.

Learning to ask—of others and of yourself—is not a sign of uncertainty. It is evidence of engagement. Progress belongs to those willing to inquire before they stagnate, and to question before they quit.

Timing, Motion, and Patience

Not every answer arrives immediately. Insight often unfolds while you are in motion—learning, testing, adjusting. Asking does not mean waiting passively. It means staying engaged while clarity develops.

Momentum matters. Stagnation dulls perception. Movement sharpens it. Often, the answer becomes obvious only after you take the first step.

Clearing Internal Resistance

Unresolved emotional tension can distort the questions you ask. Resentment, disappointment, shame, and self-judgment can make your thinking reactive rather than clear. Before direction returns, some internal weight may need to be released.

Self-forgiveness becomes part of asking well. Forgiveness for what you did not know. Forgiveness for mistakes made while learning. Forgiveness for taking longer than expected. This is not indulgence—it is maintenance. A clear mind asks better questions.

Living the Answer

Asking initiates direction, but action confirms it. Insight without embodiment changes nothing. Once you receive clarity, you must live into it. That requires alignment between intention and behavior. It requires integrity.

There is no sustainable success built on pretense. Over time, what you practice becomes visible. Your life answers your questions through your choices.

The Discipline of Asking

Learning to ask well builds discernment. Discernment builds wisdom. Wisdom builds trust—both with yourself and with others.

Ask deliberately. Ask honestly. Ask in ways that move you forward rather than keep you comfortable. Keep asking. Keep refining. Keep growing.

Because the quality of your questions will ultimately shape the quality of your success.

THE SHIFT

Asking is not a weakness. It is a skill—and like any skill, it reflects maturity when it is practiced well. Yet many capable people avoid asking because it feels like exposure. They equate competence with self-sufficiency and assume that needing input, clarification, or support undermines credibility. Over time, this belief produces isolation disguised as strength.

Learning to ask requires clarity more than courage. You must understand what you need, why you need it, and what remains your responsibility to carry alone. Without that clarity, asking feels vague, apologetic, or burdensome. With it, asking becomes precise, grounded, and effective. It strengthens outcomes rather than diluting authority.

Those who lead, perform, or operate at high levels often delay asking until strain becomes visible. By then, the request feels reactive rather than intentional. Pressure replaces discernment. Learning to ask earlier—before misalignment compounds—protects momentum, preserves integrity, and prevents unnecessary erosion of trust.

Asking is not about transferring responsibility or avoiding effort. It is about acknowledging interdependence without surrendering ownership. No meaningful success is built in isolation, no matter how disciplined or capable the individual. Asking allows effort to remain sustainable rather than silently strained.

Learning to ask is not a retreat from strength. It is a refinement of it.

⏱ A Moment in Motion

The task has grown beyond what was initially expected. Not unmanageable—but heavier. Still, hesitation lingers. The instinct is to absorb the weight quietly and push through.

The moment arrives when that approach no longer makes sense. Not because of failure, but because efficiency and clarity matter more than endurance. The request is made—measured, specific, calm.

The response is not dramatic. No rescue. Just support where it belongs.

The work continues—lighter, clearer, steadier.

The Reflection

Before moving forward, pause here.
Not to justify needing support.
Not to minimize your capability.
Simply examine how you relate to asking.

- What do you hesitate to ask for, even when it would be reasonable?
- What beliefs about strength or competence make asking feel uncomfortable?
- Where has avoiding asking increased strain or slowed progress?

- What kind of support actually enhances your effectiveness rather than diminishing it?
- If asking were treated as strategic rather than personal, what would change?

Asking does not weaken authority. It clarifies it.

When requests are intentionally made, they foster alignment. When needs are unspoken, they create friction. Asking allows resources, insight, and capacity to be directed where they are most needed.

You are not required to ask indiscriminately. You are required to ask responsibly. Discernment ensures that asking strengthens rather than dilutes progress.

This chapter is not about dependence. It is about collaboration.

Before you move on, carry this understanding forward: learning to ask is learning to lead without isolation.

And success expands when support is engaged with clarity.

Capacity to Articulate Need

Asking is not weakness. It is clarity. Refusing to ask often stems from fear—of dependence, rejection, or exposure.

This chapter strengthens the capacity to articulate need without diminishing self-respect. When asking is grounded in discernment, collaboration replaces isolation.

CHAPTER FIFTEEN

LEARN TO RECEIVE

> " *"We should be careful to get out of an experience only the wisdom that is within it—and stop there; lest we be like the cat that sits down on a hot stove lid. She will never sit down on a hot stove lid again—and that is well; but also she will never sit down on a cold one any more."*
> —Mark Twain "

Receiving as a Missing Skill

L earning to receive is one of the most misunderstood aspects of success. Many people believe success is built solely on effort, discipline, and endurance. While those qualities matter, they are incomplete without the capacity to receive—support, insight, opportunity, rest, and care.

Receiving is not weakness. It is capacity.

When you cannot receive, growth stalls. When you can, momentum multiplies. Success does not move in one direction. It circulates. And circulation requires openness.

Openness as Alignment

Opportunities rarely arrive in the form we expect. Support often appears quietly—through a conversation that reframes your thinking, an introduction that opens a door, patience offered at the right moment, or someone willing to walk beside you for a season.

These moments are easy to miss if you are overly self-reliant or emotionally guarded. When independence becomes rigidity, it blocks alignment. Learning to receive allows others to contribute their strengths while you remain focused on yours. No meaningful vision—personal or professional—is sustained in isolation.

Receiving is not dependent. It is coordination.

Releasing the Need for Control

To receive well, you must loosen the belief that everything must be managed alone. Control can feel protective, but it also limits expansion. When you allow others to support you, guide you, or challenge you, your work deepens, and your perspective widens.

This does not mean accepting everything indiscriminately. Discernment matters. Not all support is aligned. But rejecting help simply because it feels uncomfortable will keep you working harder than necessary—and growing slower than required.

Growth accelerates when effort and support work together.

Receiving During Difficult Seasons

Support often becomes most visible during adversity. When momentum slows, confidence wavers, or solitude grows heavy, connection becomes essential. Isolation may feel safer, but it rarely heals. Growth returns when you allow yourself to be seen.

There are seasons when the space around you feels small—mentally, emotionally, or physically. In those moments, learning to receive care from others—or compassion from yourself—can become the bridge back to clarity. Strength is not proven by enduring alone. It is sustained through connection.

Gratitude as Stabilizer

Receiving well includes learning how to acknowledge what is given. Gratitude keeps success grounded by reinforcing awareness of connection rather than entitlement. It creates a stabilizing effect, reminding you that progress is rarely achieved in isolation. Support, opportunity, timing, and shared effort all play a role, and recognizing that truth strengthens perspective rather than diminishing autonomy.

A sincere expression of thanks matters. Recognition matters. Appreciation does not weaken independence or self-reliance; it deepens relationships and builds trust. Success that is acknowledged openly is easier to sustain because it remains relational rather than transactional. Gratitude does not inflate ego or diminish ambition. It stabilizes identity, keeping confidence anchored in reality rather than entitlement.

Letting Go as Part of Receiving

Not everything is meant to stay. As growth unfolds, certain people, habits, roles, and patterns naturally fall away. Learning to receive fully includes allowing these endings without bitterness and transitions without resistance. Holding tightly to what no longer fits often delays the arrival of what does.

What initially feels like loss frequently creates space. Only with time does it become clear that a detour was necessary, that a role had been outgrown, or that a door closed to make room for stronger alignment. Receiving is not only about accepting what arrives, but also about trusting what leaves. When release is met with clarity rather than resentment, growth remains fluid, and progress continues with integrity.

Receptivity Without Self-Erosion

Receiving does not mean shrinking. It means trusting your worth enough to accept support without questioning whether you deserve it. It means choosing confidence over defensiveness, humility over isolation, openness over fear.

When you live with integrity, generosity returns—sometimes immediately, sometimes over time. Life responds to the posture you maintain. A closed stance repels opportunity. An open one invites flow.

The Maturity of Receiving

Learning to receive is not about collecting favors or waiting passively for good things to arrive. It is about developing the emotional maturity to allow success to circulate—to give, to receive, and to continue forward without resistance.

When you master this balance, success no longer feels like something you chase. It becomes something you steward.

And that—humility, openness, and discernment working together—is essential to sustaining your look of success.

THE SHIFT

Receiving is often more difficult than asking.

Many people can request support, resources, or recognition, yet struggle when those things are actually offered. They deflect, minimize, or rush past what they have been given. Receiving can feel passive, undeserved, or uncomfortable—especially for those accustomed to carrying responsibility alone.

Learning to receive requires trust. Not just in others, but in your own worthiness and discernment. When receiving is resisted, effort becomes one-sided. Support is offered, but not integrated. Success becomes heavier than it needs to be.

Receiving is not about surrendering agency. It is about allowing contribution to land. When support, opportunity, or acknowledgment is received fully, it strengthens connection and reinforces sustainability. When it is refused or diluted, both giver and receiver are diminished.

Those who operate at high levels often underestimate the role receiving plays in endurance. Without it, momentum is maintained through exertion alone. With it, effort becomes shared rather than solitary.

Learning to receive is not indulgence. It is completion.

⏱ A Moment in Motion

The offer is simple. Assistance without strings. Recognition without demand. There is a brief impulse to decline—to explain why it is unnecessary or premature.

Instead, there is a pause. The moment is allowed to unfold. The support is accepted without negotiation or apology.

Nothing shifts externally. But internally, tension releases. The load is no longer carried alone.

The work continues—supported rather than strained.

The Reflection

Before moving forward, pause here.
Not to assess fairness.
Not to rationalize discomfort.
Simply to notice how you receive.

- What forms of support do you tend to deflect or minimize?
- What beliefs make receiving feel uncomfortable or undeserved?
- Where has refusal to receive increased pressure unnecessarily?
- What happens when you allow support to land fully?
- If receiving were treated as a skill rather than a vulnerability, what would change?

Receiving completes the exchange.

When support is accepted with clarity, it strengthens relationships and stabilizes effort. When it is resisted, isolation grows quietly. Success that relies solely on output eventually becomes unsustainable.

You are not required to receive everything that is offered. You are required to receive what aligns. Discernment ensures that receiving remains intentional rather than dependent.

This chapter is not about entitlement. It is about integration.

Before you move on, carry this understanding forward: learning to receive allows success to remain relational rather than burdensome.

Sustainability deepens when support is allowed to fulfill its purpose.

Capacity to Accept Without Guilt

Receiving can feel more vulnerable than striving. Without intention, it can trigger discomfort, obligation, or self-doubt.

This chapter expands the capacity to receive without guilt or justification. Acceptance becomes an act of balance, allowing exchange without contraction.

CHAPTER SIXTEEN

SELF-EVOLUTION

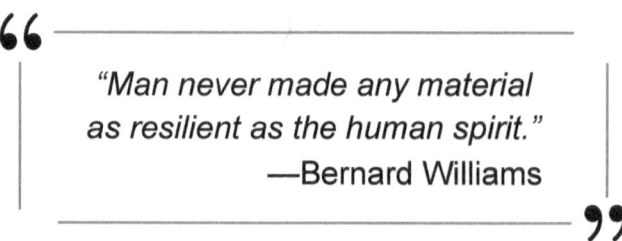

> "Man never made any material
> as resilient as the human spirit."
> —Bernard Williams

Awareness as the Beginning of Change

The look of success cannot exist without intentional self-evolution. Growth does not happen by accident. It is the visible result of awareness—of noticing how your thoughts, behaviors, and priorities shift over time. As self-evolution occurs, life begins to assume a clearer form. What once felt scattered becomes focused. What once felt uncertain becomes grounded.

Self-evolution begins when you move from reaction to intention. Awareness allows you to recognize patterns, interrupt outdated habits, and choose alignment over impulse. Over time, internal clarity begins to express itself externally.

From Performance to Self-Acceptance

One of the clearest signs of self-evolution is the transition from performative confidence to genuine self-acceptance. You stop managing appearances and begin honoring truth. External validation loses its authority as your internal compass strengthens.

You prioritize integrity over perception. When your actions reflect your values, criticism carries less weight. Approval becomes optional—not because it is irrelevant, but because it is no longer required for stability. This is not detachment. It is emotional maturity.

Stability of Self

Your look of success must coexist with a stable sense of self—one that people, circumstances, or outcomes do not easily shake. This stability marks transformation. Dependency on roles, relationships, or validation diminishes as commitment to purpose sharpens.

At this stage, you are no longer anchored to who others expect you to be. You are anchored to who you are becoming. Comfort gives way to clarity.

Embodied Confidence

Accepting who you have become is a quiet form of success. Even when others do not recognize or affirm your growth, it no longer unsettles you. Self-evolution removes the need for explanation.

You may notice changes in how you carry yourself—your posture, presence, and ease in your own body. Confidence becomes understated. Magnetism becomes natural. You are no longer trying to be seen. You are simply present.

Power, Purpose, and Focus

This stage of success is deeply internal. You feel capable, centered, and directed. Hope, patience, gratitude, peace, and belief settle into steadier states rather than fleeting emotions.

With this foundation, energy becomes purposeful. Whether you invest in leadership, creativity, service, or family, your efforts are intentional. Creative flow increases because it is no longer obstructed by doubt or distraction. Obstacles remain—but they no longer derail momentum.

The Invisible Phase of Growth

Many people enter this stage while external results lag behind internal growth. Entrepreneurs, creatives, and leaders often experience this during periods when belief has stabilized but outcomes are still forming. Financial pressure, fatigue, or uncertainty may persist—yet something essential has already shifted.

Vision becomes non-negotiable. You move forward with trust rather than force.

Transformation often feels demanding before it feels natural. Like kneading dough, change requires sustained effort before form appears. Progress occurs even when it appears inefficient. Eventually, resistance softens—momentum returns.

Recognizing Who You've Become

Self-evolution is rarely obvious in real time. Awareness often arrives later—when you realize old goals no longer fit or familiar motivations feel misaligned. Without this recognition, people continue applying outdated thinking to a new identity.

Evolution requires the release of inherited narratives, social labels, and internalized limitations. It demands honesty without self-judgment. You must see your life as it is—not as it was expected to be.

Relationships After Evolution

As your sense of self strengthens, the nature of your relationships begins to change. You start attracting people who are aligned with who you are now, rather than those who were compatible with earlier versions of you. Dependency gives way to compatibility. Connection becomes grounded in mutual respect instead of unmet need, and relationships feel less transactional and more reciprocal.

Love, in this stage, becomes mutual rather than compensatory. Growth is supported rather than feared, even when it requires change, recalibration, or distance. Generosity no longer emerges from self-sacrifice or obligation, but from security and choice. When identity is stable, connection becomes cleaner and more sustainable.

Discernment sharpens with maturity. You become more attuned to whether giving is reciprocal or exploitative, supportive or draining. Misalignment no longer demands explanation or justification. It becomes information rather than a problem to be managed.

Choosing Growth Over Comfort

Self-evolution requires ongoing evaluation. Motivations, environments, and commitments must be reassessed as awareness deepens. Opportunities may increase with growth, but not every option will align with your values or direction. The ability to choose selectively becomes a form of self-respect rather than limitation.

When you find yourself repeatedly framing your efforts as "just a means to an end," it often signals that growth has stalled. Dissatisfaction is not failure; it is feedback. When acknowledged honestly, it becomes a catalyst for change rather than a source of discouragement.

The Discipline of Becoming

True success depends on focus, integrity, and sustained self-honesty. Self-evolution is not something that is completed or achieved once. It is a discipline—one that requires continued attention, reflection, and willingness to adjust as understanding evolves.

There is no expiration on growth. The decision to become more aligned, more capable, and more intentional can be made at any stage. It is never too late to begin.

THE SHIFT

Self-evolution is not a dramatic transformation. It is a continuous process of refinement.

It happens quietly, often without announcement. Beliefs shift. Priorities recalibrate. Old strategies lose relevance. New ways of thinking take root. Self-evolution does not demand that you abandon who you were—it asks that you remain responsive to who you are becoming.

Many people resist self-evolution because it disrupts familiarity. Growth can feel destabilizing when identity has been built around consistency or expertise. Yet refusing to evolve creates a different kind of instability—one marked by stagnation rather than uncertainty.

Self-evolution is not about reinvention for its own sake. It is about relevance. What once served you well may now require adjustment. The willingness to evolve allows success to remain aligned rather than rigid.

Those who evolve consciously do not chase novelty. They refine discernment. They release what no longer fits without self-rejection. They integrate new understanding without erasing experience.

Self-evolution is not departure. It is integration over time.

⏰ A Moment in Motion

The pattern is familiar. The role is well-worn. From the outside, everything still fits.

Internally, however, something has shifted. Certain responses feel automatic rather than intentional. Decisions that once felt aligned now require reconsideration. The change is subtle, but persistent.

There is no urgency to act. Just awareness. The understanding that growth is asking to be acknowledged—not forced, not resisted.

The evolution has already begun.

The Reflection

Before moving forward, pause here.
Not to redefine yourself.
Not to discard your past.
Simply to notice where evolution is already occurring.

- In what ways have your values, priorities, or perspectives shifted recently?
- What parts of your identity feel ready for refinement rather than defense?
- Where are you maintaining patterns out of habit rather than alignment?

- What growth feels uncomfortable—not because it is wrong, but because it is unfamiliar?
- If self-evolution were treated as a responsibility rather than a disruption, what would you approach differently?

Self-evolution does not require permission from others.

When growth is resisted, tension accumulates. When it is acknowledged, coherence strengthens. Evolution allows success to remain flexible, responsive, and honest.

You are not meant to remain static to prove consistency. You are meant to evolve to remain aligned. Stability does not come from sameness—it comes from self-trust built over time.

This chapter is not about becoming someone else. It is about becoming more fully yourself.

Before you move on, carry this understanding forward: self-evolution is not a phase of success. It is the condition that allows success to continue.

And alignment deepens when growth is welcomed rather than resisted.

Capacity to Adapt Without Losing Self

Growth changes form. What once fit may no longer align. Evolution does not require abandonment of identity—it requires refinement.

This chapter refines the capacity to adapt without losing self. When evolution is conscious, success remains coherent rather than fragmented.

CHAPTER SEVENTEEN

DEFINE YOUR OWN HAPPINESS

> 66
>
> *"There is no happiness like that of being loved by your fellow creatures, and feeling that your presence is an addition to their comfort."*
> —Charlotte Brontë
>
> 99

Happiness Is an Inside Job

Happiness has always lived within you—not outside of you. Any happiness that appears to come from external sources is temporary, conditional, and often misunderstood. The belief that happiness should look the same for everyone is one of the most persistent cultural myths.

In truth, happiness is personal.

For some, it is found in partnership and family.

For others, in solitude, independence, or creative freedom.

Some thrive in structure. Others in fluidity.

There is no universal formula. Trying to live by one often leads to quiet dissatisfaction.

Unlearning Inherited Definitions

One of the most difficult tasks in adulthood is unlearning the definitions of happiness passed down by family, culture, or expectation. Many people never pause long enough to ask what joy actually feels like in their own body and spirit.

Even more damaging is the belief that another person—often a partner—should complete that definition. If you do not understand what happiness means to you, no one else can responsibly carry that responsibility.

When Expectations Collide

Conflict arises when personal truth clashes with social norms. Marriage, for example, has long been positioned as the ultimate container for happiness. Experience has shown otherwise.

This raises difficult questions:

Is it ethical to involve others in a version of happiness that contradicts your truth?

Is silence about your real desires protection—or avoidance?

Perhaps the judgment people fear is not external at all, but internal—the moment when you must face the choices you made in pursuit of joy.

Happiness and Integrity

No one knows with certainty what lies beyond this life. What we do know is that integrity matters while we are here. Living honestly—with yourself and with others—is part of defining happiness.

True happiness includes peace. It includes laughter that comes easily, joy that does not require permission, and moments that feel nourishing rather than performative. That kind of happiness is wealth.

Relationships and the Look of Success

When a relationship ends—or lingers beyond its natural life—you must ask whether it still aligns with your look of success. If it does not, the most compassionate choice may be release. If it does, it deserves renewed presence, honesty, and care.

Love does not require spectacle. It thrives in attentiveness—undivided presence, sincere words, quiet consistency. These gestures carry more weight than any display of status.

The Illusion of Surface Happiness

Luxury, excitement, and appearance offer brief pleasure, but they do not sustain joy. Once novelty fades, emptiness often returns. Happiness built on aesthetics alone cannot endure.

Petty disqualifiers—too loud, too quiet, not polished enough—often block deeper connection. When values are rooted in kindness, honesty, and emotional safety, surface preferences lose power.

The Questions Beneath the Questions

This chapter does not define happiness for you. It invites the questions you already carry.

Sometimes life answers indirectly. A person may pray for love, then resist it when it arrives imperfectly. They may seek validation while overlooking respect. The deeper question beneath the desire may be: *Am I worthy of being loved?*

Choosing Your Definition

Defining your own happiness requires courage. It requires honesty. It requires releasing borrowed narratives and choosing alignment over approval.

Happiness is not something you chase. It is something you recognize, claim, and protect. When you define it on your own terms—without apology—it becomes sustainable.

And that, too, is part of your look of success.

THE SHIFT

Happiness is often treated as a reward—

something earned after achievement is secured, stability is established, or expectations are met. In this framework, happiness is postponed, made conditional on outcomes that remain perpetually just ahead. Lived experience rarely confirms this promise.

Happiness is not an endpoint.

It is a definition.

When happiness is externally defined—by achievement, approval, or accumulation—it becomes fragile. It fluctuates with circumstance and erodes under pressure. When it is internally defined, it becomes steadier. Less reactive. More durable.

Defining happiness on your own terms does not require abandoning responsibility or ambition. It requires clarity. It means deciding what *enough* looks like. What peace requires. What fulfillment feels like in daily life—not in abstraction, but in practice.

Happiness does not demand constant pleasure.

It requires coherence.

When values, effort, and identity are aligned, happiness emerges quietly—not as intensity, but as steadiness.

Happiness, defined honestly, becomes sustainable.

🕑 A Moment in Motion

The pace has slowed—not because effort has stopped, but because urgency has softened. The accomplishments remain. The responsibilities persist. Yet something has shifted.

There is less proving. Fewer comparisons. More discernment.

In an ordinary moment—unremarkable and unobserved—a sense of contentment surfaces. Not excitement. Not relief. Just a grounded ease that comes from living in alignment with what matters now.

Nothing external has changed.

Everything internal has.

The Reflection

Before closing this book, pause here.
Not to evaluate outcomes.
Not to judge the journey.
Simply define happiness on your own terms.

- What does happiness look like in your current season of life?
- How has your definition of happiness evolved alongside your success?
- What brings you a sense of peace that is not dependent on performance or recognition?

- Where have you postponed happiness in the name of achievement?
- If happiness were treated as a practice rather than a destination, what would you honor more consistently?

Happiness does not eliminate challenge. It reframes it.

When happiness is defined internally, success no longer has to compensate for dissatisfaction. It becomes part of a larger, more integrated life. Happiness rooted in alignment remains available even when circumstances shift.

You are allowed to redefine happiness as often as life requires. Growth will demand it. Transitions will insist on it. Clarity will reward it.

This chapter is not about settling. It is about choosing well.

Before you close this book, carry this understanding with you: happiness is not found by reaching someone else's ideal. It is created by living in integrity with your own.

And success becomes meaningful when happiness is defined— not deferred.

Capacity to Choose Meaning

Happiness does not arrive as a reward for endurance. It is shaped through choice, alignment, and presence.

This chapter strengthens the capacity to choose meaning rather than postpone fulfillment. When happiness is defined internally, success becomes integrated instead of conditional.

OWNING YOUR LOOK OF SUCCESS

Owning your look of success begins with what you accept as true about yourself—your capacity, your resilience, and your ability to grow beyond prior limits. As Eleanor Roosevelt observed, no one can make you feel inferior without your consent. This truth matters not because it removes difficulty, but because it restores agency. Life will bring elevation and resistance, clarity and confusion, often at the same time. Mastery is not avoiding these contrasts, but learning to hold them without losing your center—and continuing forward regardless of season.

As this book has shown, success is neither linear nor permanent. It is not achieved once and secured indefinitely. It is shaped through time, attention, discipline, and continual recalibration. It is tested by uncertainty, complicated by money, sustained through motivation and skill, strengthened through asking and receiving, and refined through self-evolution. Along the way, its definition will change. That is not instability; it is maturity.

This moment may not feel like arrival. It may feel like an in-between—after certainty has dissolved but before clarity has fully returned. That space is not emptiness. It is a threshold. And thresholds are where recalibration happens.

You do not fail by trying. You fail only when you disengage—when you stop listening, stop adjusting, stop choosing with intention. Pause, doubt, and redirection do not invalidate progress. What matters is whether you remain actively engaged with your own life, rather than outsourcing your worth to outcomes, approval, or comparison.

If you believe life is divided into winners and losers, pause and examine where you are standing—and why. If others appear ahead of you by your own standards, consider what actions you are taking to claim your version of fulfillment. Comparison collapses complexity. It reduces layered lives to surface indicators and ignores the private costs required to sustain what looks enviable from the outside. Measuring yourself against incomplete information will always distort your sense of progress.

Waiting for external validation or permission keeps you circling the starting line. Guidance can support you. Systems can assist you. Relationships can strengthen you. But ownership is non-transferable. The responsibility for defining, pursuing, and sustaining a meaningful life cannot be delegated without consequence.

Direction rarely arrives fully formed. It reveals itself incrementally—through experience rather than certainty. The people who enter and exit your life do so within this unfolding process. Some arrive to teach. Some to challenge. Some to support growth at a particular stage. Others reflect aspects of yourself still integrating. Even loss carries instruction. Even endings orient—though their meaning often becomes clear only in hindsight.

Spend time with yourself—not in isolation, but in honest presence. Observe without judgment. Your external reflection tells only part of the story. Within you is a force that is intuitive, creative, alive, and evolving. It will surprise you. It will stretch you. It may unsettle you when familiar identities no longer fit. But it is always guiding you toward greater coherence, depth, and alignment.

Your body is not an obstacle to your purpose. You are already equipped—exactly as you are—to contribute, to create meaning, and to live with intention. Nothing about your appearance, background, or history disqualifies you from a meaningful life. Purpose does not demand perfection. It requires presence. The work you are meant to do in the world is not limited by how you look, but shaped by how honestly you live.

Time will continue to reveal the intelligence embedded within your experiences. It allows for reflection, repair, and realignment. Acceptance is not resignation. It is the clarity that makes intentional change possible. Acceptance without choice becomes stagnation. Choice without acceptance becomes resistance. Together, they form the foundation of sustainable growth.

Life is generous, though not always gentle. It responds to what you offer. Attention shapes experience. Energy circulates. Even hardship serves a function—building discernment, strength, and depth you may not yet recognize as essential. What feels disruptive now often becomes formative later.

Owning your look of success does not mean declaring arrival. It means living in alignment with your values as they evolve. It means choosing clarity over performance, sustainability over appearance, and integrity over urgency. It means allowing achievement to support your life rather than replace it.

You are allowed to redefine success as often as life requires. You are allowed to want more, to release what no longer fits, to rebuild, and to choose differently as awareness deepens. Growth will demand it. Transition will insist on it. Wisdom will reward it.

Own your look of success.

It was never something to gain from others.

It was never something to perform or prove.

It was always yours to claim—

and yours to live with intention.

Final Reflection

---◆◈◆---

What Is Your Look of Success?

Before closing this book, pause—not to measure yourself, but to orient yourself.

Success is not a fixed destination or a universal achievement. It is a personal standard, shaped by season, responsibility, capacity, and values. And unless that standard is defined intentionally, it is often inherited unconsciously—from culture, comparison, expectation, or pressure that no longer fits who you are becoming.

Whether you are imagining what lies ahead, recalibrating after decades of effort, or standing in the in-between space where clarity has not yet fully arrived, this reflection is an invitation to define success on your own terms—honestly, deliberately, and without performance.

Use the prompts below as a working framework. This is not a test. There are no right answers. The value lies in reflection, not resolution.

1. Your Current Definition

At this stage of your life, how do you define success now?

Not as it once was.
Not as it was expected to be.
But as it feels accurate today.

Consider:

- How you spend your time
- How you earn, manage, or relate to money
- How you measure progress or fulfillment
- How you experience peace, pressure, or purpose

Write your definition in one clear sentence.

My current definition of success is:

----

2. Alignment Check

Which parts of this definition feel true, grounded, and internally aligned?

Which parts feel inherited, assumed, or carried forward out of habit rather than intention?

Aligned aspects:

Inherited or outdated aspects:

----

3. Cost Awareness

Every version of success carries a cost.
Some costs are chosen deliberately.
Others are absorbed unconsciously.

What does your current definition of success require from you:

- emotionally...
- mentally...
- physically...
- relationally ....

Which costs feel reasonable and worth carrying at this stage of your life?

Sustainable costs:

Which costs feel excessive, draining, or misaligned?

Unsustainable costs:

----

4. Capacity Assessment

Success is not measured only by what you achieve, but by what you can *sustain*.

Capacity changes across a lifetime. What was possible once may no longer be desirable. What once felt out of reach may now be accessible in new ways.

At this stage of your life, what do you realistically have the capacity to carry?

Consider:

- Responsibility--
- Visibility--
- Pressure--
- Change---
- Growth--

What are you well-equipped to handle at present?

What requires strengthening, pacing, or recalibration?

----

5. Intentional Redefinition

If success were required to *support* your life—rather than consume it—what would need to change?

What would you preserve?

What would you release or revise?

What would you choose to prioritize differently?

----

6. Ownership Statement

Complete the statement below. Read it back to yourself without comparison, justification, or performance.

My look of success, at this point in my life, is defined by:

This reflection is not meant to be completed once and set aside. Revisit it as your life evolves.

The look of success is not static. It matures as awareness deepens, as capacity shifts, and as priorities become clearer.

Success becomes sustainable when it is defined from the inside out—when it reflects who you are now, not who you once needed to be.

That work is ongoing.

And it belongs to you.

The ideas explored in *The Look of Success* are part of a broader body of work focused on identity, leadership, and sustainable success in complex, high-pressure environments.

Across books, frameworks, and applied leadership tools, Dr. Karissa Thomas examines how individuals and leaders carry responsibility, navigate change, and define success beyond visibility, productivity, or external validation. This work centers on the belief that achievement without internal coherence is fragile—and that lasting success requires integration rather than performance.

At the core of this body of work is **The Mosaic Way™**, a human-centered framework for leading and living with coherence in a fragmented world. The Mosaic Way™ emphasizes three interdependent capacities:

Emotional Integrity

The ability to recognize, regulate, and respond to emotion with honesty and self-respect, without suppression or performative control.

Cultural Flexibility

The capacity to move across environments, systems, and expectations with awareness and discernment, while remaining grounded in one's values.

Identity Agility

The ability to evolve roles, purpose, and self-definition across seasons of life without fragmentation or self-betrayal.

Together, these capacities support leadership that is adaptive rather than reactive, grounded rather than performative, and sustainable rather than extractive.

Rather than offering formulas or shortcuts, this body of work provides language, structure, and reflection for those navigating ambition, transition, and responsibility. It is designed for readers who seek clarity over comparison, alignment over acceleration, and success that can be carried with integrity over time.

Each work stands on its own, yet a shared commitment to coherence, self-authorship, and sustainable growth connects all.

D r. Karissa Thomas is an award-winning author, leadership strategist, and transformational educator with over two decades of experience helping individuals define success on their own terms. Her work spans corporate leadership, education, and global professional development, supporting people as they cultivate clarity, emotional resilience, and identity-aligned growth.

Holding a doctorate in Educational Leadership and an Executive MBA, Dr. Thomas bridges research-based insight with lived experience. Her approach integrates personal development, emotional intelligence, and sustainable performance, serving leaders who want success without self-erasure.

She is the creator of **The Mosaic Intelligence Method**™, a framework designed to guide identity-rich leadership and transformation across cultures, industries, and life stages. Through her writing, speaking, and coaching, Dr. Thomas challenges conventional definitions of achievement and invites others to lead with depth, integrity, and purpose.

Her work consistently returns to one core belief: success is not a destination—it is a daily practice rooted in courage, clarity, and self-defined joy.

www.ingramcontent.com/pod-product-compliance
Lightning Source LLC
Chambersburg PA
CBHW050847150626
46549CB00012B/586